Jacques Neirynck

The Vassula Enigma

In direct communication with God?

Trinitas™

The Vassula Enigma

By Jacques Neirynck

Published by Trinitas
P.O. Box 475
Independence, MO 64051-0475, USA
Phone: 1 (816) 254-4486 • Fax: 1 (816) 254-1469
April, 2003

Cover photograph: Christian Coigny
Translated from French: Elise Bonnette, Canada

The author particularly wishes to thank les Éditions du Parvis, CH-1648 Houteville, for seeking permission to quote sections of books and other material used in this publication from their copyright holders

A special recognition for all those who assisted in publishing this edition.

Contents

CHAPTER ONE

The Beginning

My first meeting with Vassula took place on a cold gray January morning at the bar of the Beau-Rivage Hotel in Lausanne. My editor had asked me to meet with her about the possibility of publishing a volume of interviews. For this first interview Vassula was accompanied by Father James Fannan who had been the very first priest to recognize the authenticity of her religious experience.

Swiss luxury hotels are "metaphysical" places par excellence. Everything is arranged so that the guests will experience not even the slightest inconvenience and will have no excuse for not being contemplative in these cathedrals of the hotel trade. In this, the Beau-Rivage is top of the line. Greeks and Turks met there in 1923 to put an end to the war between their countries: the Treaty of Lausanne was signed in the hotel's reception rooms, but the end of the war did not mean the end of hostility. Likewise in March 1984, for the many Lebanese factions who promised to come to an understanding, but did nothing of the sort. Luis Bunuel retired to the Beau-Rivage to draft the scenarios of his transcendent films. The grounds even include a cemetery for the dogs that die at the hotel after having brightened the lives of the rich clients sojourning at this mecca.

Such a rarefied atmosphere induces a human being to meditate on his destiny, on his *raison d'etre or* his absurdity. According

1

to one's inclination, this hushed atmosphere can be transformed into paradise or hell. There I was, at 9 a.m., stirring a little spoon in a cup of coffee, wondering whether I was about to meet a saint or a witch. She was neither.

I had never heard about Vassula, except in a negative way through a Notification from the Vatican cautioning Catholics against her writings. So I expected to discover a fanatic evangelist, a New Age celebrity, or the dangerous founder of a new sect. Well, the woman I met was quite natural, more reserved than expansive, dressed tastefully yet unaffectedly, and a housewife and mother like any of the thousands we come across in the streets of Lausanne. But evidently she lives totally within an interior force. I decided to begin the series of interviews, without quite knowing where they would lead me and what I would discover.

I am not, by nature, disposed to the mystical. By training, I am wary of the supernatural, of its displays and its ruses. By experience, I know that human beings are easy prey to their imaginations, always ready to escape the monotony or gloom of their fate by looking for and welcoming prodigies and miracles.

So I strongly adhere to what Jesus said to the apostle Thomas: "You believe because you can see me. Happy are those who have not seen and yet believe." (John 20:29) In my opinion, the faith of a Christian today is based not on having seen, but on the witness of those who have seen, as related in the Scriptures. Caught up in everyday life, the average believer does not have the benefit of apparitions or miracles. He is left to himself facing the mysteries of nature, which he sees as cruel and indifferent. In times of sorrow, it seems to him that he is crying out to God for help without receiving any response. If we had to sum up in a word this century drawing to a close, what we would perceive foremost is the silence of God, never as eloquent as at Verdun, Auschwitz, Sarajevo, or Kigali.

Yet the Gospel and the golden legends of the saints relate an abundance of prodigies, signs, and wonders. Even if we cannot take them as true, word for word, the most reasonable man of the twentieth century cannot help asking himself if no historically solid proof can be obtained, it does not rule out that noticeable proofs or signs were ever given. Even if heaven does not open up for him, he cannot rule out the possibility that it may have for others, in times past and perhaps even now. The mystical experience of which he is deprived may exist, unknown to him, for others who are gifted, privileged, or more persistent in prayer. It cannot all be summarized as a universal fabrication based on deception, for mystics possess a formidable gift of acting with determination, tenacity, and discernment. The world, such as it is, has benefited equally from the martyrs' blood, the missionaries' sweat, and the contemplatives' calloused knees.

It is in this frame of mind that I listened to Vassula during the five interviews of approximately three hours each that comprise the substance of this book. They took place in her apartment. I paid the closest attention to the strange words uttered by my interlocutrix. She was introducing me to a world that I knew only by hearsay, through the accounts of the explorers of that country which lies in the innermost recesses of our souls and into which we are so afraid to venture. I, who think of angels as stylistic figures in Semitic literature, did not flinch when she spoke about angel Daniel and archangel Michael with whom she spends hours: it was something natural, like talking about acquaintances we would have come across in a Lausanne street. I, who at best will meet Jesus when I die, was talking to a woman who has been seeing Him face to face for the past eleven years: He had departed from

His traditional role as dispenser of justice to sit at our table as a companion.

It is not for me to support or to discredit Vassula's writings. I have merely been chosen as a writer. My habit of systematically questioning everything makes me an impartial observer. I do not have any serious training in theology, especially in that branch that deals with special revelations. Later on I will enumerate the criteria formulated by specialists in the field of ascetic and mystic theology. I will certainly not attempt to apply them; the matter being much too delicate. Those church authorities whose responsibility it is to rule on such questions seem to me to carry a heavy load that I refuse to assume.

Thus the reader should not expect any conclusion, positive or negative, at the end of this volume, either for or against Vassula's message. The purpose of the book is to give him or her the elements that will enable them to form their own opinion. The only thing that matters is the experience of God that they may have already had or that they will or will not have. The reader looking for extraordinary tales, breathtaking revelations, or an esoteric adventure is bound to be disappointed. A special revelation is authentic only to the extent that it repeats a message consistent with Revelation or Tradition while making it more dynamic, better adapted to our times, evoking resonances that appeal especially to the men and women of today. It may not be spectacular, but a meeting with God can only be achieved in silence and reserve.

CHAPTER TWO

Life in Egypt

J.N.: You were born January 18, 1942, in Egypt. Could you describe briefly your background? Your father's occupation...your relationship with your mother?

V.: I was born into a Greek Orthodox family. My father, who is now dead, was named George and my mother, Mary. I have two sisters and a brother. The four of us were born in Egypt, as were my father and mother. At the time there were many Greeks living in Egypt, along with French, English, Italians, and Armenians. We were living in Heliopolis, a very beautiful city on the outskirts of Cairo, built by the Belgian industrialist, Baron Empain. His statue still stands in a city park. He drew up an extraordinary plan for the city with parks, wide streets, and not very high buildings. It was really quite beautiful; a peaceful city. My mother had sent us to an English school not far from our home. A very quiet life, a family that was used to life abroad, away from Greece.

J.N.: What was your father's occupation?

V.: My father was an architectural engineer and was working in Cairo. My mother stayed at home. In those days, and especially in Egypt, women from well-to-do families did not work.

J.N.: Could you tell us something of your relations: neighbors, friends, and relatives?

V.: The whole family was there. There were my grandfather and grandmother, aunts, uncles, and cousins on my father's and my mother's sides. We always met on Sundays at my grandmother's, who was rather strict. As we say in Greek, she wanted us to put both feet in one shoe and walk with that shoe. I went to school, but was not an above-average pupil; I was rather average. I was weakest in mathematics.

J.N.: You went to primary school in Egypt. Did you pursue your studies to secondary school and college up to the level of the French baccalaureate?

V.: In 1958 my family had to leave Egypt following the change in government. King Farouk had been deposed by Naguib and then Nasser nationalized all foreign firms. My father was working for a French company. The Egyptians replaced him and my father left Egypt first, before we did. He went to Greece to look for a job. But we could not go to Greece because we didn't know the Greek language enough to be able to write it. We looked for a French or English-speaking country and my mother decided to come to Switzerland. It was like jumping by parachute just about anywhere, because we did not know where to go. My mother said that she wanted to go to a neutral country, where there was no war, because she had had enough of that atmosphere. And I did not complete secondary school in Egypt where I had two more years to go. In Switzerland I was enrolled in the College du Belvédere, near Chauderon, to learn French. Then I followed a course in a school called Hermes, which I believe no longer exists, to become a secretary. After three years I received my diploma as an executive secretary that enabled me to work in Switzerland. My father also found work in Switzerland. Around 1960 the whole family settled in Pully, near Lausanne.

J.N.: You come from a Greek Orthodox family, yet it seems that you did not follow any religious practice, since your family had none.

V.: My parents went to church at Easter time. I remember that as a child in Egypt, we went to church at Easter but not other times. When we came to Switzerland, my father went almost every Sunday to the little Orthodox Church in Lausanne, but our family did not teach us that we had to go to church every Sunday like everybody else.

J.N.: Is that normal in Greek society?

V.: Well, let's say that there are families that are more casual about it. It's somewhat normal.

J.N.: Somewhat normal?

V.: It's not unusual. But I can't say it is quite normal, because there are other families who attend church regularly. It depends on the family. In our family, anyhow, my mother prays a lot, but only at home. She believes in God and is religious but always at home.

J.N.: And she never thought of giving you a religious education?

V.: Not at all, not even the catechism.

J.N.: So, you hadn't read anything about religious matters either?

V.: No. At the time I had not even read the Bible. Except at school a little because it was an Anglican school. We sometimes read the Psalms and learned them by heart. But I did not get any basic religious education.

J.N.: It seems that you received First Communion rather belatedly. Therefore, since you did not attend church, you did not go to Communion often.

V.: We did go to Communion at Orthodox Easter. I remember we had to fast for three days before and especially on Good

Friday; we would eat black lentils, representing the Blessed Virgin's tears, with vinegar, representing the vinegar Jesus drank on the Cross.

J.N.: Even if you did not have any theological training, your family was not ignorant of the faith or hostile to religion. They were rather open-minded.

V.: Very open, but not religious to the extent of attending church every Sunday.

J.N.: It is not obligatory for the Orthodox?

V.: No, it is not.

J.N.: No other religious experience when you were young?

V.: When I was about six, I had a vision of Satan's two hands. He wanted to strangle me. I was terribly frightened and I have never been able to forget that vision. I did not know it was Satan, but I knew it was an evil force, someone very evil. I told my mother because I was very upset. Much later, when I was ten or so, I had a dream in which I saw Christ standing before me looking at me and smiling at the same time. Even as I am talking to you now, I can remember the way He was holding His head, a bit sideways, not quite facing me. He was smiling and when He saw that I was looking at Him, He said to me in English: "Come to Me!" Just as He was saying: "Come to Me!" I had the impression of being in a corridor. I felt a sort of force, a rush of air that was pulling me toward Him and I panicked because I could not control this force. I wanted to step back, but I couldn't. That force drew me to Him every time He said, "Come to me!" that force was pushing me toward Him until my face was close to His. Then the dream faded away.

J.N.: Was it the same face you were to discover much later?

V.: Quite so. Then two years later, I dreamed of a spiritual wedding with Christ. I knew I was taking part in a wedding, that He was there, that He was invisible but that it was Christ. And I was telling myself that I was not seeing Him because if He were Christ, I must not look at Him with my eyes. There was a crowd standing before us; we had to pass by them. I saw an open door. I went into that room, the Blessed Virgin was already there with St. Mary Magdalen and two other women whose names I did not know. Right away the Blessed Virgin came toward me and started to set my clothes straight, fix my hair, and make me beautiful for Her Son, so that I would be presentable to Her Son. And then it was over. After those two dreams I had no more visions.

J.N.: Those two dreams didn't prompt you to go to church, to pray? It didn't change anything in your life?

V.: No, it didn't change anything. I have often thought about those two dreams, because they were quite remarkable and today as I am telling you about them, it is as if I had them yesterday.

J.N.: Why didn't you answer the call, if it was a call, and why did you answer later, in 1985?

V.: I do not think that I did not answer. God takes His time with us. It was like a first summons before He really offered me His complete Revelation.

J.N.: Let us go back to your training that you completed with a secretarial diploma. You were then eighteen. Did you start working?

V.: Yes, I worked for five years as a secretary at the Bonnard store in Lausanne, which has since been, renamed "Le Bon Génie."

J.N.: Like your father, who was earning a living as an engineer, you had to work to earn a living. You did not belong to a family with an independent income. What cultural interests did you have when you were young? What attracted you most: reading, painting, music, or dancing?

V.: At the time it was painting. All the paintings in the room where we are sitting now are my work. I was greatly attracted to painting; in fact, everyone in my family painted, from my grandfather to my uncle. The artistic gift was in the family. When we were still in Egypt and I was thirteen or fourteen, my mother had enrolled us, my slightly younger sister and me, in a fine arts school in Cairo called Leonardo da Vinci, rather far from where we were living. It was an Italian school quite famous over there, and we attended classes for two years. We did portraits, the first year in pencil and the second year in charcoal. The third year, the year we had to leave Egypt, I would have started oil painting. I was a little disappointed that I could not finish, but once we were in Lausanne, I bought tubes of oils myself to start over on my own.

J.N.: Did you participate in art shows?

V.: I had a lot of exhibitions.

J.N.: And you are still painting?

V.: No, not at all. It's over!

J.N.: Are there any painters, classical or modern, whom you like particularly?

V.: I like only the classical painters up to Gauguin and Van Gogh. I like Rembrandt very much. I had adopted a little of his style in the beginning. Then I changed because I was tired of black as a main color. Finally I felt stifled in that atmosphere and I used only colors.

J.N.: You are not much interested in abstract art. What about music?

V.: Today, I like only classical music. Until my conversion, I didn't like it at all. Until 1985. At that time I liked only pop music.

I can't explain that. Let me tell you exactly what happened. I was aboard a plane on my way from Denmark to Thailand, because I had been living in Bangladesh for eleven years. Since I had this communication with my guardian angel, I was hearing him inwardly, speaking to me; I was seeing him internally. He wanted to form me even in such matters. He wanted me to forget all about pop music, rock music, and listen to classical music instead. And while he was talking to me he was saying: "Put the radio earphones on and listen to the piece that is about to begin; it's my gift to you." It was Schubert's Ninth Symphony, and it made a hit with me. I liked it right away and all that was on the same program. And all of a sudden, if anybody put on pop music I could no longer listen to it, it pained me. I bought a lot of audiocassettes of Schubert and other composers. I bought everything because I wanted to hear everything; it was like a craving. And I threw away all the pop music.

J.N.: Liturgical music?

V.: I'm crazy about it also.

J.N.: Orthodox music, Gregorian music?

V.: Gregorian music I like very much and also certain Orthodox liturgies, but not all. But as with classical music, there are liturgies I like better than others. There are also certain liturgical works that I do not like that much.

J.N.: Let's talk about what you read when you were young. Since you were brought up in English, I imagine you read mostly in English rather than in French. When you came here you began to read French books. Who are your favorite authors?

V.: I used to read anything.

J.N.: Isn't there some writer who touched you at any time?

V.: Ah, yes. *David Copperfield* by Charles Dickens.

11

J.N.: And among French authors?

V.: At school we had to read Moliere. I never understood anything about Moliere.

J.N.: Besides painting, which kept you quite occupied until 1985, you had other pastimes; you particularly enjoyed sports and played tennis, I think. You were quite good; it was your favorite sport.

V.: I started playing tennis early and then as I was improving I became more enthusiastic. I began taking part in club tournaments. At the end I even competed in a national tournament in Bangladesh. I had a German partner who did what I didn't do; running after the ball I didn't like, but I was good at the net.

J.N.: Any other pastimes, hobbies worth mentioning?

V.: I liked bridge very much. I learned to play bridge because in the countries where I lived, seventeen years in Africa, after all, games such as bridge made it easier to socialize. I learned to play and I liked it very much. But when I had this revelation, all of a sudden I couldn't bear it anymore.

J.N.: Anything else about hobbies?

V.: All those activities that I liked before, all of a sudden when I had this revelation, I began to prefer more serious things. It was like a change in character if you wish.

J.N.: Now, you no longer need diversions?

V.: No.

J.N.: Let's go back to the story of your life. You worked for five years, from 1960 to 1965, as a secretary at Bonnard's, and then you got married.

V.: After the wedding we left right away because my husband was working for the United Nations in Sierra Leone, the first African country where I lived.

J.N.: You had two children by that first marriage?

V.: Jan and then Fabian. My younger son is still living here because he is studying. Jan is already working.

J.N.: After Sierra Leone?

V.: It was Sudan, where my elder son was born. Then Ethiopia, where the younger was born. Then we went to Mozambique. From there I returned to Sweden for a little while where I was married for the second time. I left again for Mozambique, then to Lesotho, and finally Bangladesh.

J.N.: And your conversion occurred while you were in Bangladesh, in November 1985. Is that so?

V.: Yes, on November 28.

CHAPTER THREE

The First Encounter with the Angel

On November 28, 1985, as she began another day's work, Vassula was no different from any of the women expatriates in Third World countries who try to relieve the tedium of their exile with a social life devoted to tennis, bridge, and receptions. She was not practicing her Christian faith; besides there was no Greek Orthodox Church in Dhaka, the capital of Bangladesh, where she was living.

J.N.: On this November 28, there was no sign pointing to your conversion. You had not been affected by any special family event, emotional trouble, or premonition, absolutely nothing?

V.: That is the interesting point. Some people discover faith after a family catastrophe, when they have to cling to something. They turn toward God; they cling to God. Sometimes God wants them to come to conversion in this way, even at the cost of suffering. As for myself, at that time, it was nothing of the sort. I was not even looking for God. He was so far away. When all that happened my life was very successful. I had lots of friends. We always met at the club. Life was easy because expatriates are well paid. We had servants, chauffeurs, and guards. I had five employees at my disposal. And at the same time I was having an exhibition of paintings, and the private viewing had taken place at the Sheraton Hotel. I had decided, before my conversion, to give 25 percent of my earnings to the poor of Bangladesh. When I figured my accounts I found out I hadn't earned anything.

J.N.: You took part in fashion shows.

V.: As a hobby. I was running here and there. My mind was completely encumbered with all those things. On the morning of November 28, at around 11, I was writing down a list of things to do for a cocktail party that evening. Suddenly, I felt a presence, but all inwardly, because there was nobody else in the room. I was surprised, but also curious because it was a sensation quite different from anything I knew. I felt my hand was being taken. As if a hand was touching my hand. I was holding a pencil, and it seemed to me I was getting a little push to write. I said to myself, "Well, let's see what's going to happen." It was as if my hand was being guided. My angel had me write down, "I am your guardian angel and my name is Daniel." He drew a heart, and starting at the center of the heart he drew a rose. It's too bad I lost that first drawing.

J.N.: It is too bad you didn't keep it. Why not?

V.: It was just a loose-leaf paper and I didn't keep it because I wasn't attaching any importance to it. Well, it started that way and I told myself, "It's fantastic!" I only had to think of a question and the angel answered it. I realized right away that I had entered into communication with a mysterious being. In order not to forget the conversation I wrote down the next question. At that moment he took my hand again to answer.

J.N.: As you were writing down that dialog, were the two handwritings very different?

V.: Yes, quite. I will show them to you later. It was the beginning. That evening I told my husband what had happened. When he came home I showed him the piece of paper, "You see, I can communicate with my guardian angel." He smiled, because he always keeps both feet on the ground. And he told me, "But it's fantastic! Let me read!" He never doubted me to the point of saying: "My wife has lost her mind."

J.N.: He believed you from the start?

V.: From the first day. My ten-year-old son also; a child believes right away. And I told my tennis friends, "Do you know that something very strange is happening to me? My guardian angel approaches me and talks to me." And those girls, who were living in the same ignorance and the same whirl of activities as I, believed me right away. They were even telling me, "Vassula, if we didn't know you, we would think you were crazy."

J.N.: When you ask him his name, he replies, "Daniel." What's the name of an angel? I understand very well the significance of a man's name, or more exactly of his first name, the name given to him by his parents at birth and at his baptism, the name by which he will later be called aloud. But what's the name of an angel?

V.: I learned later that all angels, like all human creatures, have a name. My guardian angel introduced himself as Daniel. I learned much later that it means the angel of justice. And every angel has a name that has a special meaning.

J.N.: What happened after that first day?

V.: The next day, my angel came back in the same way. I spent endless hours in a state of joy, communicating with him. The following day he came back again but, to my great surprise, he brought with him a multitude of angels from the different choirs. I thought the doors of heaven were suddenly wide open because I could easily perceive this great movement of angels from above. They all seemed excited and happy, as if expecting a wonderful event. By the manner of their rejoicing I understood that all heaven was feeling festive. Then, all together, with one voice the angels sang: "A blessed event is about to take place!" I understood that whatever this event was it concerned me directly, but although I was trying to guess I couldn't find out what it was about. All day long the choir of angels sang the same refrain, allowing themselves just a few minutes of silence in-between. Each time the heavens opened up, the angels repeated the same refrain.

J.N.: At what point did the angel talk to you about God?

V.: The first words my guardian angel spoke about God were, "God is near you and He loves you."

J.N.: That was all?

V.: I must have deeply wounded the Lord at that time because the angel's words didn't have the slightest effect on me. I remember thinking, as he spoke that way about God, that it was quite normal for an angel to say this, because angels live close to God. I didn't answer and my angel didn't add anything. It was only a few days later that my guardian angel suddenly changed his attitude toward me and I noticed how grave his expression had become. In a very solemn voice he asked me to read the Word. I pretended I didn't know what "the Word" signifies and asked him what he meant. At that, my angel looked even more serious and told me that I knew perfectly well what he meant; however, he explained that it meant the Holy Bible. I already had an answer on the tip of my tongue and told him that I didn't have any at home. He asked me to go and get one. I went on arguing with him, saying that what he was asking was impossible because in Muslim countries like Bangladesh, where I was living at the time, bookstores do not sell Bibles. He told me to go immediately to the American school, which my son attended, and borrow one from the library. I was wondering if I should go or simply refuse and stay home. What embarrassed me also was how my husband and all my friends were going to react to all this. I simply couldn't imagine myself reading a Bible in front of them! I was already searching for a place where I could hide it before I took one home. Looking again at my angel's grave expression, I decided to obey him. I jumped into my car and went to the school where I found many Bibles on the shelves. I picked one, which I brought home and opened to read it, exactly as my angel had asked. My eyes fell on the Psalms: I didn't understand one word I was reading. It was a sign from God to show me how blind I was.

J.N.: *At that time you had not read the Scripture?*

V.: I had never read it.

J.N.: *Before this did you believe in angels?*

V.: I did.

J.N.: *You believed in them. You had learned about the existence of angels through the tradition of your family. You go to the American college, find many Bibles, pick one, and read a Psalm.*

V.: I didn't understand any of it and I closed the Bible. God wanted to tell me at that time, "You are in complete darkness; you see absolutely nothing." And then my angel put me through purification; I can say it was terrible but it made me understand what I really was. Thus, he began to recall and show me the sins I had never confessed. He showed them to me as on a screen. He reminded me of every event and how it had offended God. But the most severe reproaches concerned the rejection of God's gifts. My angel told me that it was a major offense to God to deny and reject His gifts. He made me see my sins with the eyes of God, as God sees them and not as we see them. They were so monstrous that I despised myself and cried bitterly. That state I was in, as I was to understand later, was grace from God in order that I repent sincerely. My sins were shown to me so clearly, crystal clear;

the interior of my soul was exposed so openly that it was as if I had been completely turned inside out. I suddenly experienced what Adam and Eve had felt after they had sinned, when God approached them in His light, facing them. My soul was unveiled, exposed. I was feeling naked, repugnant, and ugly. I could only say to my angel, between sobs, that I didn't even deserve a decent death and that, such as I was, so horribly bad, I had to die and be cut up in little pieces and thrown to the hyenas. This purification must have lasted nearly one week. I was feeling a sort of fire, a cleansing fire, purifying the interior of my soul, and it was of course a painful experience.

J.N.: In particular, you mention that the most painful offense is rejecting God's gifts. What you reproached yourself for at the time, was it your frivolous life?

V.: That, and not only that. I understood that God was giving me so many blessings that I did not want to see and that I was spurning as if they had been worthless. It caused me great pain to see truthfully the real Vassula.

J.N.: You had never been to confession?
V.: No.

J.N.: But confession does exist in the Orthodox Church?
V.: Yes, but I had never been taught about it.

J.N.: In short, you confessed to your angel?
V.: It was repentance from the heart. I cried for two weeks.

J.N.: Have you been to confession since? In which church?
V.: Sometimes with the Orthodox, sometimes with the Catholics. It depends on where I am.

J.N.: After the initial purification, the angel brings you to a first meeting with God. Can you explain how it happened?

V.: I had to suffer that purification, because my soul was so bad; it was not worthy; one is never worthy of course, but I could not, in the state I was in, meet God without serious repentance. I had to go through that phase of penance, and then I heard the voice of God the Father. I felt great satisfaction in being with my angel, but the approach of God the Creator was completely different. When I heard for the first time the Father's voice talking to me, I was really struck by two facts. First, the fatherly tone of His voice, but then you need to have met a father who takes his children and hugs them in his arms, that kind of a father. He sounded so fatherly that I was saying to myself: "But it is as if I had heard it before in my life." As if I had known Him all my life. Once, when I had to reply: "Yes, Lord" to a question, I said spontaneously: "Yes, Dad!" I got hold of myself immediately: "What am I saying, 'Dad' for God!" I was shocked because the Orthodox is very austere, very strict. And there I was calling Him "Dad," not even "Daddy." Just "Dad." I told myself: "And what is He going to say now?" And right away He answered: "My daughter, do not be afraid. I have savored that word 'Dad' as a jewel." And I felt God's joy. Even today, when I am telling you about this episode, I find myself eleven years back in time and I relive that exchange because a meeting such as that one is never completely forgotten.

CHAPTER FOUR

One God in Three Persons

J.N.: "Dad" is the English translation of "Abba" in Aramaic, the language Jesus spoke. He used this word to begin the prayer we call "Our Father."

V.: Since that day, especially when using my mother tongue, Greek, and when I am telling my sister about my meetings with God, I say *"Mao babas muipe,"* "My Daddy told me." I say it without thinking, I feel Him so much as a father.

J.N.: All those conversations that you have had then or since, were they always in English, or sometimes in Greek?

V.: No, always in English. The Lord uses the language I can best understand and write.

J.N.: You finally met God, of whom you say He is the Father; you call Him "Daddy." On your first meeting you go to the window, you show Him the wretched sight of Bangladesh and you say to Him, "Look at what the world has become!"

V.: In my ignorance and guilelessness I was telling myself: "But He is going to do something." The way it happened it was as if I had accompanied Him to the window. I show Him the sight: "Look at how those people are living, such wretchedness."

J.N.: Did God make any comments?
V.: No, not a word.

J.N.: Never, on that subject?

V.: Later, yes, but on that occasion He didn't say anything. Many people are asking me: "If God exists, why does He allow all the evil that is happening?" I have received direct answers from Mary and Jesus on that subject.

J.N.: We'll return to that later. After that meeting with God, did you try to share your experience with people who could help you? Priests, for example?

V.: I had to fight from the very beginning. I was like a child who discovers a garden full of fruits. This child starts eating the fruits. And then someone, an adult, comes and says to him: "Be careful, there are also poisoned fruits!" I felt like that child who is suddenly afraid of touching the fruits. I was happy with my conversion until that time when my angel sent me to the Dakha seminary to find a priest. The seminary stood just opposite our house. After listening to me, the priest said: "You are sick, you are schizophrenic."

J.N.: It was Father Karl?

V.: Yes, Father Karl. I had hoped a priest would understand all that was happening to me. But not at all. And then, finally, I took fright at what was happening to me. Long afterwards, Father Karl, who was a patient man, understood that I was not crazy. He began to change his view: "Maybe it is a charism from God. He sends such charisms from time to time." Finally, he sent me to Father James. The latter became my first persecutor. He told me right away:

It is satanic, diabolical. And I know what I am talking about. When someone who is suffering from cancer goes to see a doctor who discovers the cancer, the patient's first reaction is to reject the diagnosis. It is the same with you. You are experiencing satanic manifestations, period!

Well, I knew I had been converted and many of my friends also. Only God could have made us return to church and lead a spiritual life. I was very disappointed with that first contact with Father James. I went home. Then I said to God:

If it is really you, God the Father, whom I am meeting, may this priest, this one at least, not all the others, may this priest tell me one day that my messages are from God. And then I will no longer have doubts; I will know that you are God.

He replied: "I will make him bend."

J.N.: And did Father James finally bend?
V.: Yes, he did.

J.N.: Not right away?
V.: No, not right away, but I had to endure that also. I had to struggle for a long time. When Christ came to talk to me after my meeting with Father James, I sent Him away. I said: "Go away," because I was not sure about what was going on. During three or four months I sent Christ away.

J.N.: It seems that what made Father James believe in the messages was reading the texts you were writing under dictation. You showed him the texts, he read them. What struck him about them?

V.: What struck him is that there were no theological errors, since they had been written by someone like me, who had never studied theology, not even the catechism. He explained to me that a theological text is like a mine field. Only someone who knows where the mines are placed will not step on them. Theology is like that. It is touchy.

J.N.: It is touchy ground and we can easily make mistakes. Since that time have you been reading theological works?
V.: No, I do not have the time. Maybe God does not let me have the time so that I do not study and people cannot say that I am repeating what I have learned in books.

J.N.: You have never entered a formal study program, in a theological faculty for example?

V.: Nothing of the sort, absolutely nothing. Everything I receive, indeed everything I write, I have heard directly, in silence, inwardly. Besides, as you know, as an Orthodox I did not know a thing about the disputes among Catholics within the Church. Yet, the Lord was beginning to give me some information. Father James was wondering how I could know those things because I did not belong to the Catholic Church.

J.N.: Can you relate one of those details that you learned directly from the Lord?

V.: I learned that there was a rebellion, a kind of apostasy within the Catholic Church. The Lord was telling me about priests, the good priests and the others, those who rebel against the Tradition of the Church and against the pope. The Lord was then beginning to disclose all that to me.

J.N.: Did he give you names?

V.: No, no names. Never names.

J.N.: God talks to you. In fact, that is your charism. You meet God the Father, then you meet Jesus, so you have a Trinitarian vision of God; it came to you long before you knew what the Trinity represents for Christians. When you are writing under dictation, or when you are receiving enlightenments, apart from the angel Daniel, can you always discern between the Father and the Son?

V.: Since the beginning I have always been very conscious of the Three Persons of the Holy Trinity, and I talk to each one of Them and I refer to Them as three distinct persons. At the beginning, my guardian angel led me to the Father who made me feel an extraordinary and very fatherly tenderness. Later, I had a spiritual wedding with the Son who asked me to call Him Spouse, Friend, Brother and Holy Companion. Even if I call Him Father, as He allows me to do, there is never any doubt in me that He is indeed the Son, the Second Person of the Trinity. Then the Father and the Son revealed to me the Holy Spirit whom I consider as the Guardian of our soul, our Lamp, our Friend, our Banquet, our Festivity, the Pearl. The Holy Spirit is the Love that renews, revives, and transfigures our souls into columns of ardent fire so that we may be filled with zeal for God. In *True Life in God,* I speak to one person, then to the other, or I move from one person to the Trinity. The latter may tell me something, and then the Son may continue alone; then the Father.

J.N.: You are never mistaken?

V.: Of course not. The dialog begins with "Peace be with you." I know right away whether it is the Father or the Son. There is no possibility of error. There was never any confusion, even if I have been accused of mixing up the persons of the Trinity. I can't possibly mix them up, because I know who is talking. I know for example that the Father talks to me, then the Son talks to me, but at first I didn't write down that it is the Father and then at the transition that it is the Son who is talking to me. The theologian who reads all that will naturally say that I mix them up.

J.N.: But as far as you are concerned, it is always perfectly clear?

V.: Yes, quite. I would like to share with you a vision I had, for a moment, of the Trinity. On that day, I was seeing Jesus standing up while He was dictating a message. Suddenly, quite unexpectedly, I saw two other persons coming out of him, one on His right and the other on His left. All three were identical. Then, very quickly, in the same manner as they had come out they were absorbed by Jesus who was alone again.

J.N.: Are the messages different? Is the tone different?

V.: Yes. The tone also is different. In allowing me to converse with the Holy Trinity, God is trying to convey a true image of the Three Divine Persons, an image which we are beginning to lose in this century; that is, that the Holy Trinity is not a vague concept but a truly alive reality of Three Persons.

J.N.: Could you characterize the difference in tone between the first Two Persons of the Trinity?

V.: Yes, because when it is the Creator, the Father who is talking, as I explained to you before, His tone is very fatherly. He talks like a father, His attitude is that of a father, and His anger is like the anger of a father who is trying to inculcate some common sense into his children. When it comes to Christ it's different. It is Christ who is talking. I feel that it is Christ.

J.N.: As a brother, as a man?

V.: As a guide, not a man, as a Holy Companion, Christ, the Savior. When Christ talks of His love, that love is tender and has nothing to do with the external senses, sentimental, palpable. All is happening in the inmost part of the soul. On January 8, 1987, Christ approached me saying, "Be My bride Vassula." to which I replied, "How could I!" He said, "I love you." I insisted, "I don't know how to be Your bride." Jesus explained: "I will teach you to be My bride, beloved." I asked: "Do I carry a symbol for this Lord?" Then, He told me solemnly: "I will let you carry My Cross; My Cross cries out for Peace and Love." Then He tied me to His Holy Cross. It was our bond. When later I told Him that I would help Him carry His Cross and that we could share It, He was very moved and told me, "Daughter, how I always wanted to hear you tell Me this!"

J.N.: The Messiah, then.

V.: The Messiah, the Savior. Yes. And above all when He speaks of Himself as the Sacred Heart, because the Sacred Heart does not belong to the Orthodox tradition.

J.N.: You had never read anything about the saint who introduced the devotion to the Sacred Heart?

V.: No, it came later.

J.N.: Does it happen that God, when talking to you, speaks of Himself as being the Spirit, the Third Person?

V.: When the Holy Spirit talks to me it is during a dialog within the Holy Trinity. He is God, like the Father and the Son. Later on, He entered into the dialog and said wonderful things, "You do not know Me, which is why you are rejecting Me; you invoke Me but you do not really know Who I am." He gives examples. He says, "I am like earth. Come and sow your seeds in My soil to reap eternity."

J.N.: In your book, True Life in God, *there are many levels of communication. There is dictation, literally word for word, maybe kept for the more difficult, and the more complex matters which you would find hard to formulate in your own words....*

V.: Such as the Ten Commandments.

J.N.: The Ten Commandments?

V.: I received an explanation, not about the Ten Commandments but about the sins against the Ten Commandments.

J.N.: And which is the most important, which sin is the most important?

V.: For example, the Ten Commandments prescribe: "You shall not kill." God explains that Commandment at the physical and spiritual level. He says: "You are killing souls." A bad confessor can kill souls. And at the physical level, about abortion: "You are killing your child."

J.N.: By then you already had read Scriptures, you had read the Ten Commandments, or did you write them down for the first time under dictation?

V.: Yes. I had read the Ten Commandments. I knew them.

J.N.: So it is a commentary on the Ten Commandments. Have you read the whole Scriptures?

V.: No. I tried. Some of the books are very difficult to understand.

J.N.: Have you read Exodus from beginning to end?

V.: From beginning to end, yes.

J.N.: Which books in the Bible haven't you read?

V.: Oh, Maccabees, Kings, Joshua, because, you know, that's history. I haven't read the Gospels from beginning to end, but large passages because I read the Gospels almost every day.

J.N.: You never read any commentary on the Gospel? I mean exegeses written by theologians.

V.: Ah, no, never. Much later, not at the very beginning, Christ began explaining certain parts of the Bible that maybe theologians find hard to understand. So he chose a few passages to explain what they mean, especially the Book of Daniel and the Apocalypse, because He says it's relevant, in relation to all that is happening today.

J.N.: Both books belong to the same literary genre; there is, in fact, a connection.

V.: At the beginning, the guardian angel, after saying, "Take the Bible and read it!" added, "I would like you to read the Book of Daniel." But I didn't understand anything at the time. It's a book impossible to understand because of the message hidden in a mysterious form of language.

J.N.: Yes, it is very difficult to read nowadays because we no longer use that literary style.

V.: When Christ deciphers the Book of Daniel He explains it so that even a child could understand. Before He dictates the commentary He infuses my mind with insights and understanding. I am so happy at having understood all at once that I am completely ready to write. But He says, "Go slowly, I am not going to disappear now, I want to dictate." And then he dictates.

CHAPTER FIVE

The Dictation

J.N.: Those texts, which have been dictated to you and which are reproduced in True Life in God, *did you save them starting in 1985?*

V.: For the first few months I was writing them down on loose-leaf sheets that I either threw away or lost. But afterwards I wrote in notebooks which I buy in supermarkets; very simple, red student exercise books. Because for Greeks, red represents the Resurrection. Everything is written in pencil. I will show them to you. Every notebook has sixty-four pages and today we have a total of eighty-seven notebooks [107 notebooks are published as of March, 2003] plus five notebooks of dialog with the angel.

J.N.: How long does it take, when you write? Will you write for fifteen minutes, half an hour?

V.: It depends. It can be five, ten, fifteen minutes, but when it is a real dictation on an important matter, let's say the rebellion presently going on in the church, that will take time. There was a time when it took nine hours of dictation.

J.N.: In one stretch?

V.: Not at all; there were interruptions.

J.N.: According to what I've been told, if the phone rings, if there is someone at the door, you may stop taking dictation then go back to it.

V.: Exactly.

J.N.: Everything is always in English?

V.: Always, yes, always in English. It is the language I master best.

J.N.: These writings have indeed been examined by a graphologist?

V.: Yes. There were even three graphologists. The first was Mr. Munier, and then the second was Abbé Curty, and the third, Mr. Lombal.

[J.N.'s Comment:: I suggest that we reproduce here the analysis made by Mr. Munier to whom a sample of your writings had been submitted. He had been told simply that you were a forty-seven-year-old woman and that you were using two types of handwriting, without telling him that the first handwriting corresponded to dictation and that the second was your own personal handwriting. J.A. Munier is a graphological consultant in handwriting for the Court of Appeals of Paris.]

Graphological Interpretation of Mr. Munier

With no previous information and without consideration to the text itself due to the lack of knowledge of the English language.

Interpretation of the large letters:

—(Extraordinary telluric force).

—A controlled enthusiasm with a touch of delight, i.e., seems to be the source of some kind of well-being.

—She is filled with a force that goes beyond her normal self.

—She is filled with invisible forces to which she reacts with a kind of primitive simplicity, whereas there is also in other areas a refined element.

—She is convinced of this invisible power, which she perceives with intensity.

—She is an intermediary, like a center of transmission and amplification.

—She has the faith of a mystic.

—She experiences a kind of tranquil enthusiasm, a kind of fullness.

—She is very redoubled, nourished by an invisible force that seems indestructible.

—The writing, in any case, appears a bit strange from an ordinary point of view.

—She is very hard working; she is a docile pupil.

—She is in a kind of secondary state, indifferent to the exterior world.

—She can perceive invisible worlds quite well, like a medium.

—She has a very great concentrated force; she is profound in meditation.

—She does not belong to herself. There is a certain firmness. She has great self-control, probably in her demeanor as well. She is dignified.

An additional interpretation of the fragments of handwriting in smaller letters between the lines:

—She is a person who lives in her own world.

—She is not mentally ill.

—She is of at least above-average intelligence.

—She follows her own logic.

—She is capable of some integration.

—She conducts herself with tenderness, kindness, and docility.

—She has a goal and is dedicated to it.

—She experiences an inspiration from a high level.

—Her life is inspired by an ideal.

—Nothing else really matters for her.

J.N.: Besides the graphological interpretation that deals only with the handwriting was a linguistic analysis ever made? It is, for example, an analysis of the frequency of certain words that make it possible to detect differences in style, in grammatical form. What might be interesting, if it has not already been done, would be that linguists, exegetes work on it, to find paraphrases of the Bible and quotations.

V.: There is something like that being done by a Father Michael [Kaczowski], who is Polish.

J.N.: What might be interesting also, since the first texts at your disposal date back to 1985 or 1986, would be to find out if there has been a linguistic evolution, particularly through your contact with the Bible. If the messages are written by you there should be more quotations. Have you been observed by anyone during a writing session?

V.: Yes. One observer was Philippe Loron, a Frenchman who has a doctorate in psychology. He has published a book called *J'ai vu écrire Vassula* [I Saw Vassula Write]. He had an experience while I was writing because he was present. We could quote what he relates.

J.N.: Yes, here is an interesting passage.

On Monday, March 14, [1997] in the afternoon, between 2:30 and 3:30, an occasion presented itself when Vassula agreed to show me privately how she receives the messages. After a period of preparation through prayer, she gets down on her knees and asks a question in writing: "My Lord?" She then gets "I Am" in hieratical handwriting. Then comes the message, in the same handwriting. I often heard her pronounce the words before writing them, which indicates indeed an interior locution. But it is not a simple hearing, for the writing is no longer the same as hers. I have noticed a stronger constriction in the way the pencil was held straighter, which made the writing a little slower yet as fluent as the other, but more determined and pressing more heavily on the paper. I did not notice any hesitation or agitation.

Vassula is fully conscious. She is not separated from her environment. She feels a touch on her wrist; she sees the surrounding world. I can talk to her from time to time. I tried to hold back her wrist while she was writing. There was a strong resistance during hieratical writing, yet not excessive. I felt muscular tension in the forearm while pulling it either toward me or toward her, the hand continuing to write at the same rhythm. I then began to feel a strong heat in my chest and on my face. I even thought there was sweat on my forehead but when I wiped at it there was nothing.

In concluding this interview regarding the form taken by Vassula's charism, who writes more or less under dictation, I thought it would be of interest to quote a large excerpt from a book by Father Fernando Umaña Moñtoya, Vassula, an Ecumenical Charism for Our Times. *The exact references are to be found in the bibliography. This analysis distinguishes several levels of "dictation" and gives a better understanding of the phenomenon.*

1. Dictation

Word for word dictation is the form of dictation that Vassula prefers, since she hears exactly what she has to write. Sometimes while dictating, the Lord uses words she does not know and she must later look them up in the dictionary to understand. She "listens" inwardly; she can describe the tone, the feeling, and the inflection of the voice. At the same time, she feels a force that prompts her to write down what she hears. She does not lose her freedom. When she is receiving dictation, Vassula remains completely in control, in contact with the external world, with her surroundings, and keeps her personal autonomy. For example, she can stop writing to answer the phone or if the doorbell rings, then continue where she left off.

Under dictation her handwriting is vertical, clear, calm, and totally different from her normal handwriting, which is small and sloping forward.

2. Nonverbal Illumination

A second form of divine manifestation consists in receiving an interior illumination nonverbally, that is without words: it is an idea, or the understanding of something that God wishes her to write in her own words. This is a more difficult form than the preceding one—dictation—because she must make an effort to find the words herself that will best express what God made her understand before she forgets. This happens in a way similar to what was experienced by Saint Teresa of Avila who, when she had an interior illumination about *"The Interior Castle,"* had to leave the chapel in haste to write down quickly what she had received from the Lord before she forgot. This is why there are sometimes spelling mistakes in Vassula's writings, because she writes "in her own way" what God has given her as an illumination or what He has made her understand. When she forgets, or if something is missing, the Lord reminds her or corrects it immediately. She writes the first time rapidly, and later makes a clean copy of what she has written, leaving out what is more personal. When she writes the second time, neatly, God makes corrections, if needed.

3. Verbal Illumination

The third form, verbal illumination, occurs when God talks faster to Vassula and gives her a whole passage at once. Then she must hurry and write as soon as possible. In that case, Vassula writes herself. That is why there are sometimes small mistakes in the handwriting. While God is talking to her she is intimately in His Presence. Then she comes out of this intimacy and tries to write as best she can what God has shown her. [Translator's note: According to Vassula, in this instance He still guides her hand while she is writing what He has conveyed to her but does not necessarily correct her small mistakes.]

It is obvious that Vassula prefers the first way, dictation word for word, because then she is sure that every word comes from God.

Vassula's charism is a very complex one. It can be classified under the general Pauline charism of prophecy, that is the grace given to someone to communicate words received from God for the benefit of the community. In Vassula's case, this prophetic charism comprises different aspects:

1. Intellectual Vision

"With the eyes of the soul" she "sees" the Lord inwardly. She can describe Him, give details about His face, His expression, His emotions... This gift of "intellectual vision" is found often in the lives of many saints and mystics.

2. Hearing

She "hears" His voice inwardly; she can perceive His expression, the tone, and inflection, the feeling of the voice that is talking to her "in her heart."... This is the interior locution, also quite frequent, as we have said above.

3. Physical Motion

Sometimes God moves her hand to write. The motion of the hand and the interior locution are sometimes simultaneous, synchronized. At other times, the locution or illumination occurs first and then only afterwards the writing, the motion of the hand.

4. "Analogical Inspiration"

In Old Testament writings we often find God's command to "write." For example, a vision or revelation: "Write this action down in a book..." (Ex. 17:14); "Put these words in writing..." (Ex. 34:27); "...write on them all the words of this Law..." (Deut. 27:3,8); "Now go and inscribe this on a tablet, inscribe it in a book..." (Is. 30:8); "Write all the words I have spoken to you in a book." (Jer. 30:2); "Suddenly the fingers of a human hand appeared, and began to write..." (Dan. 5:5); "Write the vision down, inscribe it on tablets to be easily read," (Hab. 2:2); "Write down all that you see, in a book,..." (Rev. 1:11); "Now write down all that you see of present happenings..." (Rev. 1:19); "Then I heard a voice from heaven say to me, 'Write down...'" (Rev. 14:13), etc. Writing prophets occupied a first-order place in Biblical revelation. But Holy Scriptures are not without analogy in the life of the church; on the contrary, throughout its history we find innumerable writings that show analogical "inspiration," that is the action and presence of the Holy Spirit illuminating the writer's mind, giving it light and lucidity to "judge" correctly the things of God, and the strength and capacity for putting them in writing. The writings of the Fathers and Doctors of the Church are recognized as the fruit of a "special assistance" from God; the writings of the great mystics show us that they are not purely human works, but that they benefit from an analogical inspiration, different in each case. This is why, while it is not the same Biblical inspiration, it is a similar interior grace, a true inspiration or assistance from God in bringing it forth. Vassula's case is a very powerful example of this charism of analogical inspiration. It is an inspiration different from others in that it is not founded upon any human inquiry or initiative.

God has chosen her while she was, in contrast with others, totally ignorant of anything theological and her writings are the work of God's
direct action; it is He who formed her, taught her everything, dictates
to her, inspires her, and reveals to her what she writes.

5. "Discernment of the Lord's Presence"

In addition to interior locutions, the Lord has trained Vassula to
"discern" His Presence. Jesus manifests Himself to her spiritually, inwardly, so that she can "see Him with the eyes of the soul." But that
was neither automatic nor magical. It required on Vassula's part a per-
manent effort through which she progressed slowly, learning to discern
the living and effective presence of Jesus. The Lord has slowly "educated" her for this discernment. All charisms require this progressive
education. No charism is ever automatic or magical. There is always a
slow, difficult, painful progression. As with all charisms, God proceeds
in a human way, little by little, teaching how to refine the use of the
charisms; it is the same with the gift of healing, the gift of tongues, the
gift of discernment of the spirit, etc. Grace operates slowly, depending
on the person's degree of cooperation. That is also the manner in which
Vassula had to learn the charism of discerning the presence of the
Lord, who manifests Himself to her spiritually but in such a way that
she "sees" Him in an intellectual vision as a man, as He was present on
earth. She can discern His bearing, His features, the physical expression
of His emotions, etc. That charism of discernment of the Lord's presence is complemented by the interior locutions and the "material direction" of the vertical calligraphy. As we can see, it is really a very complex and enormously rich charism.

6. "Hieratical" Handwriting

Vassula's handwriting, when under dictation, is in a vertical script,
neat, elegant, totally distinct from her own. It is what is called "hieratical"
or "sacred" writing. It is not automatic writing. This particular element
of the writing under dictation raises questions concerning the phenomenon of automatic writing, whose origin, as is very well known, may be
subconscious or even evil. When this phenomenon occurs, the person
is driven by a strange force and writes without being conscious of what
is being written. In extreme cases of automatic writing the pencil writes
almost by itself, forcing the motions of the hand. There is nothing of
the sort with Vassula. She remains conscious, independent, and free.

She can stop when she wants, then go on or simply quit writing. It is only during the first days of the divine manifestation that her hand moved in a "quasi-irresistible" fashion, but she was always conscious of what she was writing. She is always in full possession of her autonomy to stop, to go on, or to interrupt. Sometimes, when the message is very long and time is pressing, Vassula must write in her own handwriting to save time. Later, when she copies it neatly, she does it in the way the messages dictated by the Lord are written, in a vertical handwriting. This handwriting is impressive by its beauty, its harmony, the peace it expresses, the dignity and nobility of the strokes, and the elegance of its presentation. Merely looking at it makes one feel the presence of the Spirit that inspires it. Order, clarity, restraint, and refinement are evidence of its origin. The predominant vertical dimension, as in hieratical writing, in icons, etc., shows the religious depth that permeates it. It has no rigidity, no hardness, none of the disorder, chaos, or confusion indicative of automatic writing. Vassula vanishes behind that hieratical writing, as her emotions, temperament, individuality, and character also vanish. Nothing is revealed but the presence of the majestic solemnity that inspires her; nothing is revealed but the manifest presence of the sacred.

CHAPTER SIX

Private Revelation

What is the meaning of the thousands of pages transcribed by Vassula? What value may we attach to them beyond that of simple notes written in the course of meditation? Do they constitute an account of a real dialog between Vassula and invisible beings that she calls her angel, God, the Virgin Mary?

For twenty centuries Christian churches have had to deal with such phenomena. Paul himself relates what happened to him on his way to Damascus that radically transformed him. Closer to us, Lourdes and Fatima have been the sites of apparitions that have attracted considerable crowds.

The *Catechism of the Catholic Church,* second edition, published in 1997 deals with this subject at length in the following entries:

798   The Holy Spirit is "…the principle of every vital and truly saving action in each part of the Body." He works in many ways to build up the whole Body in charity: by God's Word "which is able to build you up" (Acts 20:32); by Baptism, through which He forms Christ's Body; by the sacraments, which give growth and healing to Christ's members; by "the grace of the apostles, which holds first place among His gifts"; by the virtues, which make us act according to what is good; finally, by the many special graces (called "charisms") by which He makes the faithful "fit and ready to undertake various tasks and offices for the renewal and building up of the Church.

Charisms

799 Whether extraordinary or simple and humble, charisms are graces of the Holy Spirit which directly or indirectly benefit the Church, ordered as they are to her building up, to the good of men and to the needs of the world.

800 Charisms are to be accepted with gratitude by the person who receives them and by all members of the church as well. They are a wonderfully rich grace for the apostolic vitality and for the holiness of the entire Body of Christ, provided they really are genuine gifts of the Holy Spirit and are used in full conformity with authentic promptings of this same Spirit, that is, in keeping with charity, the true measure of all charisms.

801 It is in this sense that discernment of charisms is always necessary. No charism is exempt from being referred and submitted to the church's shepherds. "Their office [is] not indeed to extinguish the Spirit, but to test all things and hold fast to what is good," so that all the diverse and complementary charisms work together "for the common good." (1 Cor. 12:7)

910 "The laity can also feel called, or be in fact called, to cooperate with their pastors in the service of the ecclesial community, for the sake of its growth and life. This can be done through the exercise of different kinds of ministries according to the grace and charism which the Lord has been pleased to bestow on them." (Paul VI, EN 73)

951 Communion of charisms. Within the communion of the church, the Holy Spirit "distributes special graces among the faithful of every rank" for the building up of the church. Now, "to each is given the manifestation of the Spirit for the common good."

2684 In the communion of saints, many and varied spiritualities have been developed throughout the history of the churches. The personal charism of some witnesses to God's love for men has been handed on, like "the spirit" of Elijah to Elisha and John the Baptist, so that their followers may have a share in this spirit. A distinct spirituality can also arise at the point of convergence of liturgical and theological currents, bearing witness to the integration of the faith into a particular human environment and its history. The different schools of Christian spirituality share in the living tradition of prayer and are essential guides for the faithful. In their rich diversity they are refractions of the one pure light of the Holy Spirit.

The Spirit is truly the dwelling of the saints and the saints are for the Spirit a place where He dwells as in His own home, since they offer themselves as a dwelling place for God and are called His temple. (St. Basil; *De Spiritu Sancto,* 26, 62:pg 32, 184)).

Private Revelations

66 "The Christian economy, therefore, since it is the new and definitive Covenant, will never pass away; and no new public revelation is to be expected before the glorious manifestation of our Lord Jesus Christ." Yet even if Revelation is already complete, it has not been made completely explicit; it remains for Christian faith gradually to grasp its full significance over the course of the centuries.

67 Throughout the ages, there have been so-called "private" revelations, some of which have been recognized by the authority of the Church. They do not belong, however, to the deposit of the faith. It is not their role to improve or complete Christ's definitive Revelation, but to help live more fully by it in a certain period of history. Guided by the Magisterium of the Church, the *sensus fidelium* knows how to discern and welcome in these revelations whatever constitutes an authentic call of Christ or His saints to the church.

Christian faith cannot accept "revelations" that claim to surpass or correct the Revelation of which Christ is the fulfillment, as is the case in certain non-Christian religions and also in certain recent sects which base themselves on such "revelations."

The attitude of the Roman Catholic Church is therefore quite positive as regards charisms. However, she leaves to the "pastors of the church" to sort out supernatural phenomena and decide what is worthy. It is understandable that the first reflex of a bishop who is confronted with apparitions in his diocese would be extreme cautiousness, if not systematic suspicion. The seer or seers must be put to the test if we are not to consider as sacred anything and everything. The Catechism is silent about specific criteria for discerning the authenticity of a private revelation.

We borrow from a list of criteria in the works of Fernando Umaña Moñtoya listed in the bibliography.

The Church has a series of criteria for discernment that must be studied and applied to Vassula's case in order to be able to form an opinion about her message.

Briefly, those criteria are:

1) Concordance with the traditional Faith as it has been upheld, explained and interpreted by the Catholic Church throughout the centuries. Likewise, concordance with Holy Scriptures as interpreted by the Church; there can be no contradiction with the latter.

2) Concordance with the doctrine and traditional moral standards of the Church.

3) The presence of objectively convincing (and proven) signs confirming the declarations of the "seer" or of the person benefiting from so-called supernatural manifestations. Likewise, for the canonization of saints, although the heroism of their virtues may have been established, miracles (signs) confirming their holiness are required. Naturally, the question here is not to canonize Vassula but to observe the obvious signs—physical and spiritual healings, liberations, deep and lasting conversions—associated with her ministry.

4) The verification of those signs, which must be, as far as possible, scientifically proven, as is the case with miraculous cures, in Lourdes for example.

5) The existence of spiritual results: conversions; prayer life; receiving the sacraments, especially the Eucharist and Penance (confession); lasting changes in lives not attributable to emotionalism, whim, fanaticism, etc.

6) Obedience to the authority of the church, especially the Magisterium and above all acceptance of the pope, his teaching, and his role as Vicar of Christ.

7) The personal situation of the "seer": a saintly way of life resulting from the supernatural phenomena he or she is experiencing; veracity and rectitude in his or her entire conduct; psychological and spiritual stability; indifference toward financial matters; respect, order, transparency, harmony in his or her entire behavior.

8) Humility, no desire to "show off." Simplicity, modesty, transparency in the "seer's" entire conduct.

9) Depth of the "seer's" doctrine, consistency of this doctrine with the life of the "seer"; not trivial or superficial.

10) Striving for charity, for unity; absence of sectarianism, exclusiveness, individualism, clannishness. Finally, the exclusion of anything that implies division, disunity.

11) The presence of the "fruits of the Spirit": love, joy, peace, patience, kindness, goodness, fidelity, forbearance, temperance, etc.

12) The absence of exaggeration, perturbation, anxiety, violence, disorder, dejection, vanity, jealousy, envy, discontent, bitterness, stubbornness, hysteria, nervousness.

The reader will keep these concrete criteria in mind when reading this book further. It will be his responsibility to juxtapose them with what he learns of Vassula's activity in order to forge his own opinion.

CHAPTER SEVEN

Vassula's Allies

*J.N.: Let's talk about your relations with the church, or more
precisely with the churches, since there are many. You gave an
inkling of the situation when we were talking about Father James
[Fannan]. You have met other priests, among them Father [René]
Laurentin. Was Father Laurentin convinced right away?*

V.: First let me repeat the instructions the Lord had given me:

"You are not to spontaneously communicate the messages to
priests or bishops. They are the ones who will invite you. Then
you will go to them." So I never approached Father Laurentin to
try to convince him or any other priest. My duty consists only in
passing on what I receive. Up to now I have never tried to convince those who are not asking anything and do not come on their
own.

*J.N.: Yet you went to that seminary opposite your house in
Dakha.*

V.: Yes, but at the very beginning, in order to introduce my-
self, before I was given this special instruction in the messages.
After that I didn't do it again. I was not to put myself forward
with the messages, especially now that I am in Switzerland where
I have many opportunities of meeting priests. With Father
Laurentin it all started because someone had sent him photocopies

of *True Life in God* before the books were published. He took some interest in the texts. Professor Patrick de Laubier arranged for a meeting at Father Laurentin's. It lasted from three in the afternoon to eight at night. He recorded the interview on a cassette and, by his own admission, he asked me some trick questions. My French was not very good at the time so I didn't answer too well. But he was finally convinced by the honesty of my answers to his questions and also by the fact that I had avoided all the traps he had set. I didn't know how to go about having a book published and he arranged himself for L'OEIL Publications to start publishing the messages. Later the Éditions du Parvis continued what L'OEIL had begun.

J.N.: How did you meet Father Michael O'Carroll who is presently your spiritual adviser?

V.: I had been invited to the United States, to Pittsburgh, to give a lecture. The lady who had organized the lecture put me in touch with Father O'Carroll in 1990 or 1991. When I was in Ireland for a series of lectures, he let me use the auditorium of his college after reading some articles by Father Laurentin. He attended the lecture and heard everything. He was convinced. Since then he has been counseling me spiritually.

J.N.: Where is he living at present?
V.: In Dublin.

J.N.: You telephone or write each other?

V.: Until now we had always been traveling together, for years, in spite of his age. Now he wishes to settle down and do no more traveling because of his fatigue and his age; he is eighty-six.

J.N.: Have you met leaders of the diocese where you reside, Lausanne, Geneva, Fribourg? The bishop for example. Have you ever met Monsignor Mamie?

V.: No. But he was negative from the start. Apparently he does not believe what I live, without having heard me. I am not wanted. I have also asked to be heard by Cardinal Schwéry. My confessor, Father Nicolas de Bulle, wanted me to meet the bishop of Sion, Monsignor Schwéry, who was later to be made a cardinal. He asked him to meet me, if only for a few minutes, before going into retirement. Cardinal Schwéry flatly refused.

J.N.: Have you met the new bishop, Monsignor Grab?

V.: I've met him. We had lunch together with Patrick de Laubier whom he knew when he was auxiliary Bishop in Geneva. On that occasion I even asked him if I could hold a meeting just the same in Geneva, in a building loaned by the Capuchins. He told me: "Do it, but not too often in the same place."

J.N.: So as not to create an unofficial parish?

V.: No. At the time, I thought that he was afraid the priests of his diocese would blame him. I can say that Monsignor Grab has always been openhearted. But I do not want to rush the clergy or insist. He is open. Let's say he has never been negative toward me.

J.N.: Any contacts with Monsignor Bürcher, the bishop residing in Lausanne?

V.: Only once. I met him by chance at a cocktail party on the occasion of the visit of the Ecumenical Patriarch of Constantinople who was passing through Lausanne. Monsignor Bürcher met me and told me: "I pray a lot for you." This was after the Notification from the Vatican warning Catholics against my testimony.

J.N.: You have never met Cardinal Ratzinger?

V.: No, never.

J.N.: And John Paul II, you have met him?
V.: Several times.

J.N.: Several times, under what circumstances?
V.: The first time in a public audience in Rome. And another time. The third time, I met him in a smaller audience. I had brought all my books that had been translated into Italian, to give to him. We asked the guards to give them to him.

J.N.: Someone was with you?
V.: Yes, Father O'Carroll. The pope passed by; he stopped in front of us and I gave him the books. I told him: "I am Orthodox. I have organized Orthodox prayer groups who pray a lot for unity."

J.N.: You have never corresponded with John Paul II?
V.: No.

J.N.: No other correspondence with the Vatican?
V.: With the Vatican, myself, never. But the priests who support me, yes. None of the letters that have been sent on my behalf have been answered.

J.N.: What parish do you attend?
V.: The Orthodox Church in Lausanne. I am a member of that church. The priest is very kind to me. He likes me. But at the start, when I arrived in Lausanne I went to this priest to tell him what was happening to me. He told me very simply that such things were beyond him and that he could not help me. Since that time I haven't said anything to him about my experiences.

J.N.: Have you received support from other sources at the international level?
V.: For example, Most Reverend Frane Franic, archbishop emeritus of Split and Makarska. In a letter dated November 15, 1995, he writes:

Before God, I declare herewith that Mrs. Vassula Ryden deserves not to be condemned but to be praised for her books in view of the integrity of the faith which they contain, especially as regards the complete primacy of the Roman Pontiff, the Blessed Virgin Mary, the true Presence of Christ in the Eucharist, the Sacred Hearts of Christ and the Blessed Virgin Mary Immaculate, etc. In her books titled *True Life in God*, all of which I have read attentively and which to date number seven, no doctrinal error is to be found.

J.N.: Any other testimony of that nature?

V.: That of Archbishop David Sahagian, Chancellor of the Armenian Patriarchate of Jerusalem, who wrote me the following letter:

It is for us an occasion of great pleasure and personal satisfaction to recognize in you a new catalyst of spiritual rejuvenation, capable through the books which you publish, to speak to our generation in a most persuasive language. Your inspired mission, which is to bring to others the message of Christ, is for the church a source of deep joy. And your tireless zeal, drawing its vigor and finding its strength in your Greek roots, is for our tormented youth an enviable example of devoted fidelity. We are proud to encourage your ecumenical mission and to pray for your success.

J.N.: Another testimony from a bishop?

V.: That of Bishop Montrose of Stockton, California:

Truly, it would not be appropriate for me to make a judgment on the writings of Vassula Ryden and I submit anything that I say to the judgment of the church. From a personal standpoint, I can only state that what I have read in the first volume of *True Life in God* has been of real benefit to me. These writings have given me new insights into the incredible love that Jesus has for me personally, and for each one of us. They have led me to a greater faith and trust in that Divine Love. I hope and pray that many others will also be blessed by reading *True Life in God*. (August 1992)

J.N.: Do you have a written testimony from Father Laurentin?

V.: Yes. He wrote a little book called *When God Gives a Sign*. He says this:

This is not a personal question for me. It is true that I have a great esteem for Vassula. It is also true that I see her as quite advanced in her spiritual life and myself small in comparison (though she humbly says that she is not a mystic but loved by Christ only for her poverty).

However, though I attach a great value to the conversions that the Lord has brought about through the faithful instrument that she has become, my personal life has not been marked by her messages. I get too many of them for one to become my "cup of tea" or my basic nourishment. That does not mean that I have not read them (as some have said to discredit me; for the opponents, surprised by the fact that I had not "seen" their objections, think that I am quite ignorant).

Though my way of analysis has its limitations, I have made a serious study. Vassula always remains open to information and objections, which I have unceasingly taken note of and examined without being polemical in dialog with the opponents.

I admire the degree to which reading or listening to Vassula has reinvigorated the spiritual appetite of so many undernourished Christians. But for me, my personal life has been nourished for too long by the basic readings; the Gospel, the sacraments and the example of the saints. So much so that no particular message is, for me, an event or plateau, not even Medjugorje, where I definitely admire the work of God. In this regard I am quite in agreement with Archbishop Fortier of Sherbrooke who says:

"The origin of all true Christian spirituality remains the Word conveyed to us by the Liturgy, the writings of the Fathers and the Doctors of the Church, and the spiritual authors approved by the Church." (His critical article of March 22, 1992 titled: "Mrs. Vassula Ryden, 1942-   .")

As we have said, private revelations have a more modest position in the Church, but they have a prophetic role that is valuable, especially in times of apostasy, tepidity, and the social and cultural strangulation of the faith found in our own times. It is then that God raises up prophets that he has always chosen in a surprising way.

This personal and legal distance that I have is another guarantee of my objectivity. However, it does not stop me from appreciating a breath of fresh air, the transparency, the perseverance, the force of love for Christ, and the power of the witness of Vassula.

J.N.: Do you wish to quote another text?

V.: Yes, that of Father Ljudevit Rupcic, a Franciscan and professor of exegesis in Sarajevo:

Vassula is a true prophet of our times. On the one hand, she deals with the problems and the needs of our times; on the other hand, she seeks new prospects from God, to come finally enriched from her difficulties and find in Him harmony, peace, and fullness. Her message is imbued with the Gospel. Its special feature consists only in the way of transmitting it to us; besides, Vassula offers to the old and new problems of our world nothing but the everlasting Gospel.

Vassula is, like all other prophets, convinced of the truthfulness of her message and the authenticity of her mission. She knows her own weakness but she resolutely keeps to her commitment to diffuse the messages to others. She finds God's help in continuous prayer and in the Eucharist. Persevering in her will and desires, she strives to be entirely united with God.

Vassula's experience with God is a lasting and inexhaustible spring of wisdom, love, enthusiasm for God and the salvation of the world. For that reason the testimony is convincing, joyful, and stimulating. Besides conversion and a call that humankind should answer love with love, there is also concern for church unity. Everywhere in her writings we feel the breath of Love. Grace flows everywhere; the Holy Spirit is everywhere at work, giving profusely.

Vassula's writings are an echo of the Gospel. The One who speaks is, indeed, the very Word of God. Vassula does not tell anything that God would not have already told, but God's Word is brought up to date through her mouth, giving prominence to priorities and needed emphasis. In this way the Word is actualized, serious, convincing, a testimony.

The question: "Why repeat what has already been said?" means that one does not know the needs of humankind, who have the right to hear God's Word in an understandable, updated way. Besides this, there is an obligation to become a messenger of the Word, which gives testimony within human experience.

Despite the objective authenticity of Vassula's testimony, people, here and there, raise objections to its truth. Though they are not sufficient to call the testimony in question, the reasons are both of an objective and subjective nature. Reservations arise mainly from a narrow and fragmentary view of the mystery of grace, especially when grace is poured out gratuitously, grace whereby God makes the human person a partner in His life and of His works. All these objections amount to human notions and language because they come from a limited human experience, unable by its limitations to accept the mystery of God. Hence man questions the Word of God and refuses to accept God. For the skeptic the Word of God is always too difficult, even "scandalous," and consequently taken as untrue.

If people faced the reality of love in God and in men, they would be led to love God and one another. If people answered the request for prayer, the message would spread throughout the world the note of thankfulness to God. If one accepted that there must be unity between the Christian Churches, already there would be a hope of the fulfillment of Jesus' promise—"one fold and one Shepherd." (John 10:16) If people accepted God the way Vassula recommends, He would already be "everything in everyone" (1 Cor. 15:28). If people took seriously Vassula's warning about Satan, the latter would already be banished from men's hearts and from the world. If people would heed Vassula's call to conversion, all men and women would be saints already.

J.N.: You still have many more testimonies from personalities who support you. It is now time to have a look at the other side of the coin, the attacks to which you have been subjected.

CHAPTER EIGHT

Opposition and Denunciation

On October 23, 1995, the Italian edition of *L'Osservatore Romano* published a Notification by the Congregation for the Doctrine of the Faith, dated October 6. Here is the English translation:

> Many Bishops, priests, religious, and lay people have sought an authoritative judgment from this Congregation on the activity of Mrs. Vassula Ryden, a Greek Orthodox residing in Switzerland, who, in speech and in writing, is spreading in Catholic circles throughout the world messages attributed to alleged heavenly revelations.

> A calm, attentive examination of the entire question, undertaken by this Congregation in order to "test the spirits to see whether they are of God" (1 John 4:1) has brought out—in addition to positive aspects— a number of basic elements that must be considered negative in the light of Catholic doctrine.

> In addition to pointing out the suspect nature of the ways in which these alleged revelations have occurred, it is necessary to underscore several doctrinal errors they contain.

> Among other things, ambiguous language is used in speaking of the Persons of the Holy Trinity, to the point of confusing the specific names and functions of the Divine Persons. These alleged revelations predict an imminent period when the Antichrist will prevail in the Church. In millenarian style, it is prophesied that God is going to make a final, glorious intervention which will initiate on earth, even before Christ's definitive coming, an era of peace and universal prosperity. Furthermore, the proximate arrival is foretold of a Church, which would be a kind of pan-Christian community, contrary to Catholic doctrine.

> The fact that the aforementioned errors no longer appear in Ryden's

later writings is a sign that the alleged "heavenly messages" are merely the result of private meditations.

Moreover, by habitually sharing in the sacraments of the Catholic Church, even though she is Greek Orthodox, Mrs. Ryden is causing considerable surprise in various circles of the Catholic Church. She appears to be putting herself above all ecclesiastical jurisdiction and every canonical norm, and in effect, is creating an ecumenical disorder that irritates many authorities, ministers and faithful of her own Church, as she puts herself outside the ecclesiastical discipline of the latter.

Given the negative effect of Vassula Ryden's activities, despite some positive aspects, this Congregation requests the intervention of the Bishops so that their faithful may be suitably informed and that no opportunity may be provided in their Dioceses for the dissemination of her ideas. Lastly, the Congregation invites all the faithful not to regard Mrs. Vassula Ryden's writings and speeches as supernatural and to preserve the purity of the faith that the Lord has entrusted to the Church.
Vatican City, 6 October 1995.

This Notification is unsigned which is against the rules. A systematic survey of the Acts of the Holy See for the past thirty-five years has not revealed any unsigned document. We may therefore ask ourselves whether that Notification was really authentic at the time, or whether this unusual presentation reflected hesitations or objections within the institution, with nobody willing to take the responsibility for the text. Who initiated the process leading to this warning?

One of the objections listed shows curious ignorance on the part of the unknown author. Certainly Vassula participates in the sacraments of the Catholic Church, but in doing so she is in perfect agreement with a rule of Canon Law: "Catholic ministers may licitly administer the sacraments of penance, the Eucharist and anointing of the sick to members of the oriental churches which do not have full communion with the Catholic Church, if they ask on their own for the sacraments and are properly disposed." (Canon 844, § 3). Therefore, according to the rules of the

Roman Catholic Church itself, no one can hold it against her. The text alludes to an "irritation" in the Orthodox Church that never manifested itself officially.

The text contains nuances implying that this is not an irrevocable condemnation: Vassula's writings and teachings are not forbidden, contrary to what occurred on numerous occasions in the case of eminent theologians such as Yves Congar, Henri de Lubac, or Hans Küng. For lack of true doctrinal errors in the definitive version of these writings, the Notification asserts only that they are not supernatural.

However, the recommendation to the bishops to ban the spreading of Vassula's message is fraught with practical consequences for the movement of spirituality that she has initiated. Many Catholic faithful will retain of the Notification what they will have read in their newspaper, that is, a blunt statement in the manner of: "The Vatican condemns Vassula."

This warning is indicative of the Vatican's persistent uneasiness when faced with private revelations. At first, the Catholic hierarchy tries to maintain a position halfway between approval and condemnation. The risk of an early approval is naturally that there may be manipulation involved: a lot of people may simulate apparitions or revelations for gain or just personal publicity. On the other hand, premature condemnation leads to painful review. Without going back to the trial of Joan of Arc, we may recall a much more recent occurrence of the same kind.

On March 6, 1959, there appeared a Notification clearly condemning the revelations of Sister Faustina Kowalska, of the Institute of Our Lady of Mercy, who had died in 1938. The following passage is unequivocal: "The spreading of images and writings which present the devotion to Divine Mercy in the form proposed by the said Sister Faustina must be forbidden." This document is hereby signed by Monsignor O'Flaherty, a prelate of Irish origin. He became famous during World War II by courageously hiding in the Vatican escaped allied soldiers sought by the Nazis.

On April 15, 1978, there appeared a second Notification which cancelled the first and from which we extract a significant passage:

This Sacred Congregation, in view of the numerous original documents which were not known in 1959; taking into account the profound change which occurred in the circumstances; and considering the opinion of many Polish bishops declare that the prohibitions contained in the said Notification (of March 6, 1959) are no longer binding.

This Notification was signed by Cardinal Seper and Monsignor Hamer.

It was only a first step before the beatification of Sister Faustina Kowalska by Pope John Paul II: it is not without interest to note that Sister Faustina had lived in the Diocese of Cracow of which [the then] Karol Wojtyla had been the bishop. Finally, on November 30, 1980, [Pope] John Paul II promulgated the encyclical *Dives in Misericordia*, inspired by the teachings of Blessed Faustina.

The conclusion to be drawn from Sister Faustina's tribulations is clear: a Notification is a provisional document that does not in any way entail the infallibility of the Magisterium.

On the other hand, a Notification acts as a brake on the spreading of documents or the organizing of meetings in Catholic churches. Such was indeed the objective of this Notification from the Vatican, issued at the request of the Swiss bishops who held great reservations about Vassula from the time of her arrival in Switzerland.

As far back as December 1989, the Episcopal Council of the

Diocese of Lausanne, Geneva, and Fribourg issued "Remarks concerning messages to Mrs. Vassula R." The document begins by acknowledging the very positive elements in Vassula's messages that are consistent with the attitudes advocated by the Roman Catholic Church with regard to prayer, Christian unity, the role of the pope. Reservations are voiced, however, on two points: on one hand, the possible confusion between Vassula's private revelation and the Revelation entrusted to the Church; on the other hand, a generalized suspicion in her revelations regarding the loyalty of priests and bishops. In its conclusion, the document accuses Vassula's messages of creating a "parallel ministry." It recommends not putting places of worship or parish halls at her disposal, as this might lead Catholics to believe that Vassula has received official approval. On the other hand, it does not object to Vassula giving her testimony at prayer meetings as long as she places herself on the same level as other participants. To sum up, the document does not so much object to the contents of the revelations as to the special status Vassula might obtain through them, a status similar to that enjoyed in English-speaking Protestant countries by many lay "preachers" who have no special training or mandate.

Two years later, in September 1991, the Diocese of Sion issued a similar warning:

> Private revelations, received without discernment by other recipients seriously threatens the credibility of the Church in their eyes. They risk giving precedence to (and often privileging) such revelations over the teachings of the Church.

On another level, the document questions Vassula's activity for Christian unity,

> The "ecumenical" behavior of V.R. is too ambiguous. Now, with and despite the difficulties and hopes of ecumenism, all the denomina-

tions engaged in dialog loyally wish to affirm what they confess. Confusion will not bring forward unity. For the time being every Christian is necessarily a member of a specific Church.

This attitude was reaffirmed in 1995 by Father Roland Trauffer, the secretary of the Conference of Swiss Bishops, who declared in a letter addressed to the director of a movement of spirituality in the United States:

> We think it sad that Mrs. R. should arouse emotions in the United States. How much time is lost with phenomena that have little to do with the Gospel! It is regrettable.

The Swiss bishops' attitude is therefore quite clear and firm. The Notification of October 23, 1995, from the Vatican was issued at the request of the Conference of Swiss Bishops, as revealed by Father Trauffer in an interview given to the Catholic News Services on November 8, 1995.

> We wanted to avoid having to reply constantly to requests from parish priests. We are very happy with the declaration from the Congregation for the Doctrine of the Faith because, now, there is no doubt that bishops must forbid her and her followers the use of parish buildings.

Vassula's rejection, first at the local level then at the level of the universal Church, was announced without the person in question having been asked to explain herself. Likewise, the priests who support her have not been questioned. It is a condemnation based solely on the writings without giving the person directly involved the chance to defend herself. It is not so much a case of summary proceedings as of an absence of proceedings.

The Notification of October 23, 1995, has naturally provoked an outcry from the priests, theologians, and bishops who support her. It would be tiresome to publish all those protests, most of which are in the form of letters addressed to the Congregation for the Doctrine of the Faith. Let us limit ourselves to that of Father Christian Curty, exorcist for the Dioceses of Avignon and Marseille at the time and presently for the Diocese of Lyons. It is dated January 28, 1996, and is a good summary of the position of Vassula's supporters:

> I am astonished and perplexed at the procedure followed by the Sacred Congregation for the Doctrine of the Faith with regard to this matter.
>
> Usually the Roman Curia, and especially your Sacred Congregation, handles such cases with a great deal of respect and kindness toward the persons subject to their judgment and in accordance with the requirements of the Code of Canon Law (particularly Articles 220 and 221). We still recall the surprising patience and delicacy used especially with regard to Fathers Schillebeeck and Boff.
>
> But in the present case, instead of Canon Law, has even the Spirit of the Gospel been respected? Was it really so urgent and was there such grave danger to faith and morals as to compel a departure from the usual methods of reaching a judgment—which is very close to being a condemnation—against Mrs. V. Ryden's faith, her communion with the church and her writings, without giving her any forewarning? Is it true that she learned of her condemnation in the press? without giving her any opportunity to defend her cause and without even questioning the many Catholic priests who know her, especially her spiritual director, Father O'Carroll?
>
> Being an exorcist priest, I have often encountered face to face the enemy, the real Antichrist, and I am painfully accustomed to hearing from the mouth of the liar and the rebel "messages" which bear no resemblance to that which Mrs. Ryden receives.
>
> Having also a degree in graphology I have followed closely the "ways" to which the Notification alludes and I have carefully studied the script of the messages of Mrs. Ryden.
>
> Now then, there is neither a relationship existing between this handwriting and automatic writing or between this content and that of messages from spiritualists. The messages of Mrs. V. Ryden have a remark-

able doctrinal vigor, are consistent with the Bible, and have a spiritual loftiness that one never finds in spiritualists' revelations.

Therefore, independently of the personality of Mrs. V. Ryden, her moral and Christian (Orthodox) conduct, which Father O'Carroll can speak to you about, and in order to address myself strictly to the messages which she says she receives from Christ Himself, allow me to submit my conclusions to you.

I deliberately leave aside the hypothesis of an ingenious and perverse deception, the content of the messages being far beyond the capabilities (literary or theological) of Mrs. V. Ryden.

In all unusual manifestations (mystical or pathological), three possibilities are open for discernment:

- **Diabolical Origin**

  To be totally ruled out! Because the evil spirit cannot persistently imitate or counterfeit the voice of Christ. And the Devil would not risk inviting the divided Church to reconcile in Unity under the primacy of Peter, much less stressing the vital importance of the Eucharist.

- **Psychic Origin**

Either from **para-normal state**

—studies of the "ways" (in terms of Scripture, circumstances, etc.) completely rule out the phenomenon of a medium or of a trance.

Or from **subconscious state**

—this presupposes the subconscious of a genius with extraordinary theological intuitions (which surpass the memory "pool" of the recipient) as well as a harmonious, constant and flawless logic.

To my knowledge, such has never been found. Moreover, this subconscious, far from turning inward upon itself, remains constantly open to a mysterious Being whose personality in no way reflects what we know of Mrs. V. Ryden, but on the contrary, bears striking resemblance to Christ and the faith of the church.

Could the subconscious be capable of carrying on for any length of time an architectural construction of such great literary beauty and of such profound theological doctrine?

This leaves:

- **Supernatural Origin.** This one compels us (for a number of reasons, I cannot elaborate here) and, I would add, summons us. For if it is really the Lord speaking to His Church, we cannot allow ourselves to treat these messages with contempt or indifference, being content with a quick and superficial reading, much less rejecting them, for which we would then be answerable.

These messages are centered not on Vassula personally, who is only the instrument and the messenger, but rather on the _Mysterium Fidei_ and the _Mysterium Ecclesiae (Mystery of faith and Mystery of the Church)._ At the heart of the message is the primacy of "Peter" *(note: it refers to primacy not Peter)* is in danger. And you know better than I of the incessant and dangerous upsurge of debate and confusion endangering the Body of the Church. This word, which comes from above, invites us insistently to reconciliation of the entire church, One in the heart of God but divided among and by the disciples of Christ. A gesture is requested (as was sought by Pope Paul VI) to celebrate together, on the same day, the Pasch of the Lord. If we accomplish this small step, the Lord will do the rest.

Your Sacred Congregation believed that it had to take a position on these messages! But there is one question that arises: We, the priests of the Catholic Church (and bishops—many outside of France) who have believed in these messages and believe that they come from the very mouth of the Lord, are we really in error? And are we disobedient to the church for believing that we recognize the voice of our Master and our Pastor who is inviting us to conversion and to Unity of Faith "so that men may believe"?

Are we still in communion with the church when we perceive in these writings not a call to a "pan-Christian community" but an invitation extended to the whole church, divided in its members, to gather under the one shepherd's staff of "Peter." Also, forgive my audacity, but would it not be necessary to appoint a commission to study in a serene and objective manner the writings (published and unpublished) of Mrs. V. Ryden; a commission, which would, in all fairness, question this person herself. Too many Christians are indeed troubled by the Notification of your Sacred Congregation which gives no precise justification for its judgment and is thus profoundly hurting their sensibilities of the Gospel teachings and wounds their faith in Christ Jesus in whom they believe and whose voice they still believe they hear throughout these messages! ...

What remains to be done is to question Vassula herself as she confronts a solemn condemnation and a storm in the media, which she did not expect.

J.N.: What is your attitude faced with this rejection?

V.: The rejection does not affect me really. Because I am sad one moment and then it goes away quickly. Sad because they do not see the truth. They do not see God passing before their door and they close the door in His face. But their rejection does not affect me. It is as if it were coming toward me and passing over me. I have said, and keep on saying:

I didn't choose this charism. I have nothing to do with it. I didn't choose to be what I am now. I haven't chosen that way at all; it is God who gave it to me. I know that this work is His and that since it is His, He will take care of His work. If this were a way that I had chosen myself I would have been completely annihilated, not by the Notification, but long before by all the persecutions I've had to endure. But the more they persecute me the more my faith grows. Even after the Notification, I contemplate God's power. I can't get over it. He had told me, "The more they persecute you, the more I Myself will make your road straight."

J.N.: Do you feel that among those who have condemned you there are people who have never met God personally and who, having built a purely intellectual image, are unable to recognize Him when He reveals Himself as He is? Wouldn't that be deep down the origin of that misunderstanding?

V.: Yes. Father Edwin O'Connor, of Notre Dame University, Indiana, wrote an analysis of what happened. He doesn't blame anyone; he doesn't criticize those who have condemned me. He tries his best to explain why those who judge me cannot see that my revelations come from God. They are reticent because my writings are on the mystical level, while they judge as theologians. So they scrutinize the texts as if I were one of their pupils. They flunk me because I am not using theological language; the language I use does not stick to their language.

J.N.: Do you feel bitter toward your persecutors?

V.: It is normal that I should have opponents, enemies. If I am bitter, it is because their persecutions impede conversions that would have come about. But the more I have been persecuted, the clearer the importance and greatness of God's call became in my mind. So, I leapt with joy when I was persecuted because then I understood the worth of the treasure that God had entrusted to me. Ever since the beginning of these revelations I expected opposition. From the start the Eternal Father had informed me that I would become Satan's favorite target, his number one target. But the Father immediately assured me that He would always stand by my side and give me His strength. He reminded me that He is known to have overthrown kings and kingdoms so that His Word be heard and that He would do the same for His work, *True Life in God.* Here are a few words from the Father that I would like to quote as they have been given to me:

You will be reared by Me and formed in My Courts; this is why you will be contradicted in your journey. The world will spit on you, but not more than they spat on My Son; traitors will come your way, but none of them greater than Judas; denials and rejections, too, will follow, yet none of them more severe than the rejections and denials that My Son received; pitilessly you will be misunderstood by many, but rejoice! Do not fall into distress, make no resistance and do not turn away either; allow yourself to be repressed as My Own Son, your Redeemer, was repressed, scandalizing all His disciples. I command you to remain untouched by the insults of men and not to respond, as My Son did not respond but remained silent—and in these sufferings I will establish peace; in your torments I will console the disconsolate; I will make your oppressors oppress you and while you will be lying down in torments, trampled underfoot by men, I will be setting light in the church, giving birth to a renewal in My Spirit Thrice Holy, surrendering her to become One. (September 6, 1995)

Condemnation or not? It's hard to know. On May 10, 1996, Cardinal Joseph Ratzinger, Prefect of the Congregation for the Doctrine of the Faith, came to Guadalajara, Mexico, to preside at the Conference of Latin-American Bishops. At his behest, four persons were received by the Cardinal after they had handed over to him copies of *True Life in God* in Spanish. According to their report, Cardinal Ratzinger told them the following:

We only want you to proceed with discernment—do not take as the word of God what is considered, for the moment, only human and personal. What we have said is that she should not witness in churches (inside the church) because she is an Orthodox and her marital status is not yet clear, being divorced; and there are in her writings some points which need to be clarified which we are studying. You may continue to promote her writings, but always with discernment. In the words of St. Paul in his letter to the Thessalonians, "Do not stifle the Spirit, do not despise prophecy, but test everything—hold on to what is good."

If this testimony is true to reality, the Notification which opens this chapter would have been published in 1995 without enthusiasm by Cardinal Ratzinger, which explains the absence of his signature and consequently deems this document invalid.

The unfolding continued in February 1997, with the publication of the Notification in the official collection of the Acts of the Vatican. This time the document was no longer anonymous but was signed both by Cardinal Ratzinger and by the Secretary of the Congregation for the Doctrine of the Faith, Monsignor Tarcisius Bertone, with a date of October 6, 1995. Yet, Monsignor Bertone was only named Secretary of the Congregation on February 3, 1996. Therefore, his signature, antedated as of October 6 (1995), appears suspect to say the least. What would be the value of such a document in a civil court, first published without a signature and then with the signature of a clerk who was not in office at the time? We cannot avoid feeling that Vassula's work causes internal controversy within the organs of the Catholic Church, leading to anonymous or antedated documents disavowed in private conversations.

Another clue is to be found in a strange expression that may have passed unnoticed by most readers of the Notification. At the end of the fourth paragraph, the Notification accuses Vassula of promoting a "kind of pan-Christian community, contrary to Catholic doctrine." One would look in vain in the dictionary for the word "pan-Christian" so we must turn to etymology to guess what the text means: since the prefix "pan" means "all," "pan-Christian" must therefore mean "all Christians." Is it reprehensible to promote the community of all Christians? Certainly not. But describing this effort with this bizarre word casts suspicion on the endeavor. The adjective "pan-Christian" made up in such a context would aim at making suspect Vassula's mission in favor of Christian unity which we will discuss in Chapter Thirteen.

But there is another explanation for the use of this convoluted expression. By November 10, 1994, John Paul II had published the encyclical Tertio Millenio Adveniente in preparation of the Year 2000 Jubilee. In it he used the contentious word to promote a "significant pan-Christian meeting." The use of the same adjective one year later to castigate Vassula is therefore quite remarkable and probably deliberately intended. If such a power struggle exists within the Vatican between the supporters and the adversaries of the unity of the churches, the October 1995, Notification may have been aimed beyond Vassula, at the persevering efforts of John Paul II in favor of the same cause.

[With permission from the author and the original publisher, Trinitas, has added the following important update and clarification of the position of the Vatican in regard to Mrs. Vassula Ryden and the messages she receives from God published under the title *True Life in God.*]

Trinitas notes that the Notification of October 23, 1995, that addressed Mrs. Ryden and these published works was a warning <u>and not a condemnation</u> as many people were falsely led to believe. The following public statements by Cardinal Ratzinger make the Church's position in this matter very clear.

In October 1997, while introducing Vassula in Brasilia, Brazil to a crowd estimated at around 20,000, Auxiliary Bishop Joao Terra revealed another occasion on which Cardinal Ratzinger characterized the Notification as being considerably less than it appeared on its face. The Portuguese Catholic magazine reported the following remarks by Bishop Terra that were recorded in their entirety on videotape:

I would like to say a word of thanks, as auxiliary bishop, for the joy that we are experiencing through the presence of Vassula here in Brasilia. Certainly it is an extraordinary grace…this year we had the regional meeting of bishops with the Holy Father. I asked about Vassula. Cardinal Ratzinger said "I have been getting a mountain of letters from cardinals."…[This was regarding the October 6, 1995 unsigned Notification published in *L'Osservatore Romano.*] Bishop Tielbeek from the Diocese of Formosa (Brazil) then asked him "But Cardinal, should I change my attitude?" Cardinal Ratzinger answered "Continue as you have done until now, but be prudent."

In the Catholic Publication, *30 Days*, No. 1, 1999, Niels Hvidt interviewed Cardinal Ratzinger on Christian prophesy. His last question was directed around Vassula. [Quoted with permission from www.hvidt.com]

Hvidt: This last question could be a little embarrassing. It regards a contemporary prophetic figure—the Greek Orthodox Vassula Ryden. She is considered by many faithful, and by many theologians, priests, and bishops of the Catholic Church to be a messenger of Christ. Her messages, which have been translated into thirty-four languages since 1991, are known throughout the world. The Congregation for the Doctrine of the Faith has, however, declared negative on the issue. The 1995 *Notification* on the obscure points as well as the positive aspects of her writings was interpreted by some commentators as a condemnation. Is that the case?

Ratzinger: You have touched on a very problematical issue. No, the *Notification* is a warning, not a condemnation. From the strictly procedural point of view, no person may be condemned without a trial and without being given the opportunity to air her views first. What we say is that there are many things that are not clear. There are some debatable apocalyptic elements and ecclesiological aspects which are not clear. Her writings contain many good things but the grain and the chaff are mixed up. That is why we invited Catholic faithful to view it all with a prudent eye and to measure it by the yardstick of the constant faith of the Church.

Hvidt: Is the procedure to clarify the question continuing?

Ratzinger: Yes, and during the clarification process the faithful must be prudent, maintaining a discerning attitude. There is no doubt that there is an evolution in the writings which does not yet seem to have concluded. We must remember that being able to set oneself up as the word and image of the interior contact with God, even in the case of authentic mysticism, always depends on the possibilities of the human soul and its limitations. Unlimited trust should only be placed in the real Word of the Revelation that we encounter in the faith transmitted by the Church.

CHAPTER NINE

God: Love and Humor

J.N.: Your charism consists in writing under God's dictation. Nowadays, people often like to hear about God since many others ignore Him completely, denying He exists, denying the existence of the Creator, denying the existence of the Incarnation, denying the existence of the Holy Spirit, and moreover, this involves unbelievers and Christians alike. Tell us about the God whom you meet.

V.: There are many people in the world who talk about God without ever having met God. It's not their fault. When Christ came to me for the first time to talk to me He said regarding my ignorance, "Could it be that no one taught you?" He wanted to allow me an excuse then. It was true. I didn't have anyone to teach me who Jesus is, what He really is. Today, if the world apostatizes, if the world does not know God, it is because people do not know what He is really about. They go to church only because they have been told they have to go, out of obligation, to be on good terms with the church, but without love. But that is not what it is about. Today, God wants to express Himself through His messages; He wants to manifest Himself in a way that can be understood by anyone. God is a person, not an abstract principle. A lot of people, even among Christians, imagine God in an abstract way, situated somewhere in His glory. Is He listening to me? Is He not listening to me? Is He seeing me? Is He not seeing me?

J.N.: It is the God of philosophers.

V.: Of philosophers who are distant, far away from God, totally distant. Even people of good faith are misled. For example, I know many Orthodox, who go to church, they light a candle, cross themselves, talk to God, but they do not really know if He listens or not. There's a kind of abyss between them and God. And then these same people, when I see them, when I organize meetings, they hunger to hear more about God. Why are they coming to hear always more or less the same words? It's because they hunger to hear, over and over again, that God is a divine and real person; that God the Father truly is a father, but more perfect than any human father. And an abyss of love, an abyss of mercy. And when I tell you the experiences I underwent... He has not given me these experiences without a purpose. He gave them to me so that I can tell people how He is, how He is at the very moment when I am repeating His words. Then people feel that God is living, that He is there by our side, that He is just like a person and that He allows Himself to be moved; so sensitive is He. As Jesus has described Him to me once, in a formula that I like very much, "My Father is a King, yet so motherly, He is a Judge, yet so tender and loving. He is the Alpha and the Omega, yet so meek." When I talk about Christ, when Christ comes to me, He comes as Savior, He comes and He is our Holy Companion. He tells me He is always near me. Whatever I do, He is always with me. If I were asked to choose, I would prefer being always in contact with Him, praying and listening to Him. But I have lots of things to do at home, I have to cook, to vacuum, I have to wash this, to do that. And so Christ looks at me and says,

Listen, do it for Me. Everything you are going to do, offer it to Me. But do it with love, for Me. And those little tasks that mean nothing to you will become great in My eyes if you do them with love.

J.N.: All mystics say the same. Service to your neighbor is not different from service to God.

V.: The Holy Spirit comes as a Lamp, a Guide, as a Companion also. I would like to quote from *True Life in God:*

The Holy Spirit will be the light of your eyes, the motive of your being, the movement of your heart, the utterance of your speech, your laughter, and your joy, the kingly ornament of your soul, the watchman of your spirit; He will be your brother, your sister, and your faithful friend; He will be your festivity, your banquet, the hidden treasure, the pearl, your hymn to the Hymn, your amen to the Amen; the promised land and the foundation of all virtues on which he will inscribe His Holy Name. (January 9, 1996)

J.N.: I am struck by the literary quality of this text. Yet you are a painter rather than a writer, visual rather than verbal.

V.: I am not a writer. It does not come from me when the Lord invites us to know the Holy Spirit better, because that is where the key is to be found. The Holy Spirit is the Heart beating within the Church.

Come closer to Me and I will breathe in you Immortality, reanimating your soul to move, aspire, and breathe in My Glory so that you no longer belong to yourself but to the One who moves you in union in Our oneness, the Trinity. (January 9, 1996)

I also wish to add that, when the Lord calls, when He manifests Himself in this way, I am not the only one in the world. There are many others now, in our times, who hear the same message. God has decided to save us, because He sees everybody falling headlong into apostasy that comes from rationalism. By constantly trying to over explain things we become so rationalistic that we lose our faith.

J.N.: What does the word "rationalism" represent for you, a doctrine, a philosophy, for example, or a word that just happened to come along?

V.: No, nothing just happens to come along. Christ Himself dictated it to me. He told me, "Rationalism gave birth to atheism. It is the enemy of the Church."

J.N.: For you the word "rationalism" has that meaning?

V.: Yes. I know friends of mine, who are very dear to me but who do not want to believe because they want answers to all the mysteries. They have no sense of mystery. They say that none of it is true and finally they build up their own philosophy. It's useless to try to convince them. It is always God's grace that converts, not us. They need our prayers.

J.N.: I would like to ask you something on that subject. You have received a particular grace that not everyone receives. Yet you have said during our previous conversation that, in any case, God presents Himself to all human beings.

V.: In one way or another.

J.N.: One way or another, because, otherwise, it would be quite unjust?

V.: Of course. But we can be blind and also not want to see that God is with us.

J.N.: Not wanting to. But is there a difference between not wanting to see and being blind? Does it mean failing to see, not understanding that a religious experience exists? When I talk with certain people, such as friends who are nonbelievers, they tell me they have never met God. It makes me feel uneasy and I wonder if it is really possible.

V.: I cannot guarantee anything, but I do not believe that the God I know could ignore some people and look only at others. He gives His grace but maybe they have pushed it away. I meet quite a lot of people who complain. Yet, we should always praise the Lord, because all that we are is already a blessing. It is a grace. You come home, you have a roof over your head, you have a fridge, you open it and you have lots of good things too eat, and you never praise the Lord enough for all that He gives you. He can take all those things away from you as He did with Job and leave you naked and sick. But He does not do it because He loves you. So that already is a sign and it is ungrateful not to recognize that God is with us. My friends and yours who say that God does not exist, they are not looking; they are not opening themselves to the sign. Why do they not open their eyes and see that everything they have, life and health, are already a sign of God? If they do not discover God, they should ask themselves a few questions. The Lord tells us, "Find Me in purity of heart, in simplicity of heart, in holiness, by replacing evil with love, by helping the oppressed, by seeking justice."

J.N.: You said a little while ago that many people talk about God but have never met Him. Were you alluding to those whose function, whose vocation it is to explain God, such as priests or pastors, who speak in churches, churches that are nonetheless becoming more and more empty? Do you feel they are becoming empty because they talk about God without knowing him?

V.: I must say that unfortunately there are many priests who have not met God. And why? A sign of this is that their churches are empty. If they had met God they would have recognized Him and, as I'm going to explain to you, the church would be full. Because every homily that comes out of that priest's mouth will be guided not by his spirit, not by his own light, but by the Holy Spirit. God gives us an easy key, intimacy. Without that intimacy we cannot meet God and know Him. We must surrender completely; go to Him like a child, and talk to Him with our heart. Prayer cannot be simply read. It must come from the heart, forming a dialog. And it is this dialog that is missing. Through dialog we meet God. Because when we make an effort at dialog, God sees that we want to meet Him. He does not stand with arms folded, letting those who are praying come up to Him. Not at all. He will run to meet you and give you abundant graces to help you meet Him and know Him...

J.N.: Except for those times of spiritual darkness that are trials?

V.: Of course. I've been through these trials many times. And I know that when I'm going through these trials of the night of the soul, it is awful. But I hope they will not go on for too long.

J.N.: What does the word "poverty" in relation to God suggest to you?

V.: Personally, when I understand the word "poverty" in a spiritual sense, it means poor in spirit, spiritual divestment. When you say that someone is poor in spirit it does not show up in clothing; it is not worn-out shoes. Poor means to be completely empty and let the space be filled by the Holy Spirit, and not filled with our own selves! If we are full of our own selves, we are rich. A wealthy man can be a millionaire and yet poor in spirit because he is following completely the way of Christ. He is empty of himself instead of being full of himself; the Holy Spirit lives in him.

J.N.: For example, George Soros, one of the world's richest men, who at a certain time caused the devaluation of the pound sterling and made a profit of billions of dollars, but now uses his money to rebuild his country, Hungary. Can someone like George Soros be poor in spirit?

V.: He can be poor in spirit. The exterior does not count. He must also be simple; simple and without malice, like a child, and innocent at the same time. Simplicity. God is simple also. And He says in His messages, "I am not complicated, you have made Me complicated, I am not at all complicated."

J.N.: You are a little wary of intellectuals?

V.: It is not that I am wary, but I am sad and I think it's a pity because after all they are also children of God. They are so intellectualized that they intellectualize God. When we intellectualize God we go further and further away from Him and love grows colder. And what do we get in the end? We are not going to live on earth forever. They think as if they were going to live here forever. They build their philosophy and when they die none of it remains. But it is the soul that lives on and it is the soul that counts afterwards.

J.N.: What do you think of those who are called Doctors of the Church? I am not talking about spiritual doctors such as John of the Cross for example, but thinkers like Augustine or Thomas Aquinas who tried a synthesis between the philosophy of their time and theology? They are considered as saints. Were the efforts they made useless or even dangerous?

V.: I cannot answer that, unfortunately. I have not read them.

J.N.: I would suggest now that we consider a question that you must have been asked often. It must absolutely be dealt with because everybody asks it. It is the problem of evil. I am not talking about the evil men commit. It is quite clear that when man commits an evil deed other men suffer from it. However, creation as we know it, involves the suffering of innocent children. Even animals suffer. Even before the appearance of man, this creation seemed very hard, extremely cruel. Sometimes people, even believers, say that if they were God they would not have created the world as it is. Of course we must never suppose that we are God. But the question, even badly formulated, remains.

V.: All right! I went to dine once with people who asked me that question. They would have liked me to find an answer to that question. If God really exists why do we live in such chaos? I didn't know what to say then. It was in 1987. When I got back home I asked Christ, "What should I answer?" His voice was very sad, and also a bit stern, grave, and sad. He did not speak long; He said, "If you are dying, it is because of your apostasy." I would like to read to you what the Blessed Virgin told me on the same subject.

The world is dead to love. It lies in deep obscurity because hatred, greed, and selfishness dominate the entire earth all the way to its core. I am shaken by terrible sights, with the iniquities of this dark world, and the apostasy that penetrated into the sanctuary itself. The disasters, famine, afflictions, war, and plague, all these are drawn by you; all that comes from the earth returns to earth; the earth is auto-destructing itself and it is not God who gives you all these disasters, as many of you tend to believe. God is Just and all Merciful, but evil draws evil. (May 15, 1990)

J.N.: So the origin of evil is finally...

V.: It comes from us.

J.N.: It comes from us. Absolutely everything?

V.: Much later, on reading the Bible I found a passage that said: "Everything that comes from the earth returns to the earth" meaning that if we did only good things and were good persons there would be none of what causes problems.

J.N.: I understand. Still, let's go back in spirit to the times before the appearance of man, let's say five or ten million years back, before our ancestors could be responsible for anything. There were already animals. Among them some were carnivorous and some were herbivorous. The lions or their ancestors eat the gazelles. It's no fun for the gazelle. To be eaten by a lion constitutes a good definition of evil for a gazelle.

V.: You eat chicken?

J.N.: Yes, I eat chicken.

V.: For you, it is not evil?

J.N.: No, it's nature. I don't know...

V.: I understand. Jesus ate meat. There is no wrong in that. But nature means also that God creates man free, of course, because otherwise he wouldn't be a man but a robot. So He gives him the possibility of committing evil. And man never missed a chance—far from it.

J.N.: Why? Why create nature with the possibility of committing evil?

V.: It is good that God gave us freedom. But man has misused his freedom. He has disobeyed and lost God's grace. God could have created man without freedom, but He would not have gotten any satisfaction from it Himself. It's a much greater glory if we give ourselves to God and go to Him. He has shown us from the start where evil lies. We recognize it in our conscience. If we are thinking of killing someone, we know very well that we are committing evil. And we choose. We choose; God does not impose anything on us. He gives us many graces, many chances to convert and go toward Him. If man rebels, he destroys himself. And we must not forget either that Satan exists. He is a person and also a spirit. It is not an abstract concept. I am sometimes being accused of speaking the language of the Middle Ages! Satan? People laugh and say that he does not exist and that hell does not exist! According to them we create hell within us and hell exists only on earth. According to them, we can spend our hell on earth or our heaven on earth. So all those places do not exist for them. But they do exist. Purgatory exists. Hell exists. Heaven exists. Satan exists. The fallen angels exist; they are the devils. God and the angels exist.

J.N.: I always come back to the same question. God created the world. Well, we should be more accurate. God is not immersed in time. He does not create the world at a specific moment. He is perpetually creating it, at this very moment when we are talking together. He supports the world if you wish. But this world is a world of suffering. Let's agree with your intuition that all evil comes from man. This is what is expressed by the theological theories on original sin. Why does God create a world in which man, a free being, necessarily introduces evil?

V.:   I am not a theologian; I have followed the path of the mystic. I know that suffering purifies the soul. The saints worried if they did not suffer enough. To be able to understand this, we must first know and love God. Then we need to understand that suffering is one of the greatest graces we can obtain. But I can tell you what God repeats to me, "I have created you out of love, to be loved." Out of His great love He has created us to be loved. We love Him and He loves us. It's a circle. It's simple. It's only that.

J.N.:   Even knowing that at the moment He is creating us to love Him, this would be done through all kinds of sufferings?

V.:   He knows everything from the start. He taught me to offer Him my sufferings. Once when I was complaining about my sufferings He told me: "If only you knew what I am offering you, you would come to Me and beg Me for more trials!" He taught me that suffering purifies the soul.

J.N.:   When God meets you, He introduces Himself by simply saying, "I Am." With these words He replied to Moses who asked him his name. So the God whom you meet is indeed the God of the Bible?

V.:   Yes. And whenever I invoke God, whether it is God the Father or Jesus, I have the answer right away interiorly. As soon as I call Him He answers and not once has He refused. He doesn't answer like my son, absentmindedly, when I call him. God says, "I

Am." Each time He says, "I Am." Some people who know me argue that for me it's easy because I have a charism; I call him, He answers, and I listen. Whereas for others, there is only silence; they do not know if God answers or not. I say that He answers because He has given me so many signs. When I was traveling with my friends—do you want me to tell you?

J.N.: Of course.

V.: There was a young Orthodox girl who was traveling with me through Holland by bus. We had to go from one meeting to the next, here and there, and she was accompanying us. As we were riding in the bus I put on the earphones of my Walkman to listen to hymns. This young girl is sitting beside me and she is holding an Orthodox rosary. On each bead you say the Jesus prayer, "Jesus Christ, Son of God and Savior, have mercy on me, a poor sinner." All of a sudden, she looks at me and smiles. And I look at her and smile just because she was smiling. I didn't know why she was doing that. When I removed the earphones she tells me: "But what you have said is extraordinary. But how were you able to utter it?" I said: "What?" She says: "I was praying and on the third bead as I was saying, 'Jesus Christ Son of God,' you were looking straight ahead and you said, 'I am' with such majesty!" I replied to her: "But I didn't say anything!" She replied: "But yes, you did say it! I heard it. It was majestic!" The evening before she had told me that it was easy for me, that I only had to call to Jesus and He answered right away, "I am." But she always doubted whether someone was listening to her. Jesus answered her the next day with this word that He said using my mouth. As soon as you invoke God's name He is there. He says: "I am standing very close and my ear is pressed to your lips," so eager is He for our words.

J.N.: Do you think that there are human beings that God prefers?

V.: It is written in the Bible that God has no favorites. He treats everybody equally.

J.N.: You often speak about God's voice. You hear Him. Of course if we tried to record Him then we wouldn't be recording anything. So it's not a word that is carried through vibrations of air, as when we are talking.

V.: It's another voice inside, quite different.

J.N.: Which you hear in your brain?

V.: He talks to me in my heart.

J.N.: You also speak about visions. Evidently, if we tried to capture it on film or on a photograph we wouldn't see anything at all. You are the only one who is seeing something. Do you see the angel, or Jesus, or Mary in the room you are standing in, or do you see them in your imagination?

V.: I think that the correct word for those visions is imaginary, yes. But that does not mean that I am imagining something that is not there; it would not be the right interpretation of the word imaginary. To describe what is really happening, the simplest word I can find is "interior," although it is outside of me. I see inwardly, with closed eyes, someone who is outside of me. I do not have to open my eyes because I do not see with my eyes. I see with my heart.

J.N.: You have said that Jesus' face coincides with that of the Shroud of Turin. Is it really that face?

V.: It is just like the face of Christ.

J.N.: In the Christian iconography of the first two or three centuries, Jesus is always represented as a beardless young man. And then, from a certain moment on, the classical representation of Jesus as a young and bearded man becomes the norm. One interpretation of this change in the way of representing Jesus is that the Shroud was rediscovered, displayed, and used as a general model. So you see Him with that face?

V.: Yes. Always the same face, of course. But the expression depends on the message He is giving. For example, once I saw Him with a claret red cape, like satin, and a gold crown on His head. A King. He had come as King to give me a message. And I was saying to myself: "If only I always saw Him as King, because I do not want Him to suffer, mystically." Once He came; He was even leaning on the wall as if He was clinging to it and He was just as if right after the scourging. And He was suffering, He was panting and perspiring and blood was running down on Him. And I was shocked. I said: "But what is the matter with you? Why are you like that?" He replied: "It is because of sinning souls that I am like that. You must pray for them." That was the message He wanted to give me.

J.N.: It is the Christ of the Passion.

V.: Sometimes His Presence around me is so strong, while remaining invisible, that when He bleeds sometimes I look in my notebook because I am afraid the blood will stain it.

J.N.: Apart from this royal vision and outside of this vision of the Christ of Passion, generally speaking, Jesus shows a peaceful, kind, smiling face?

V.: Quite so. He is then wearing a white tunic. I would like first to tell you an anecdote. I was expressing to Jesus my surprise that painters always represented Him as a stern or suffering man, never as a smiling man. Jesus replied: "It is true. I smile only on pure souls who love Me." Here I would like to use something that is already written to express myself better. Today, God is calling to us and He uses every possible means to call us to Him. He reveals His Image powerfully—who He is—because He sees that we have completely disfigured His Image, turning His Image into an abstract image. We have intellectualized Him. It is a major reason for our estrangement from Him and our present apostasy. During my public testimonies I try to depict the gift God has offered me, which is to give people as detailed a description as possible of my experience with Him; that is, of the way God approaches a soul, the way He takes care of a soul, the personal relationship He wants to have with every one of His creatures, and how He bends all the way to us to adapt Himself to us. So I try to communicate to humankind how I felt God; I have experienced His goodness, His love, His humor; in a way, His personality. Often, when the Eternal Father approaches me, He makes me feel His joy and often His humor. One evening in Bangladesh, while awaiting our guests, I was counting plates, napkins, etc. I thought I had everything on my tray. I hesitated and asked, knowing Jesus was with me, "What do we need more?" He answered me without hesitation, "We need love, Vassula." It was love and humor at the same time.

J.N.: You mention one of God's attributes, humor, about which theologians hardly talk. Could you say a few words about God's humor?

V.: Humor comes from God. I'll start with nature. There are animals that at times are very funny to observe. You cannot say that the creator of those animals does not have a sense of humor. For example, I have even seen birds that looked like hens, in Chile, that were truly bizarre. They looked funny when they walked. I burst out laughing and said to myself: "Whoever created that bird has a sense of humor like nothing else." So, already in nature, as a person, too, God shows a sense of humor, but holy humor. I'll give you some examples. Not so long ago I was hungry. I was alone in the house and I hastened to the kitchen and opened the cupboard to make myself a sandwich in a hurry because I felt that the Lord was calling me. I was telling myself: "I have to eat fast enough before I get that call because it will take me all day to write it down." At the very moment I was talking to myself, I opened the cupboard and said: "I'm hungry." And right away I heard His voice asking me, "for my word?" He was teasing me. He knew very well that I wanted to eat. But He took me by surprise and I didn't know what to say. Of course His Word is very important; of course, more important than the food we eat every day. To teach me the importance of the Eucharist, He came once when I was hungry and told me: "Will you write?" I answered: "Yes." He asked: "Are you hungry?" I answered: "In fact I am right now." And He asks me majestically: "And always hungry for My Bread?" Right away I understood that He meant the Eucharist. So I told Him: "But Lord, I was talking about the other bread." And He told me: "I know, but which is more important, your bread or Mine?" I thought a little and said, "Both!"

J.N.: It is a humorous reply for someone who has a sense of humor. It may sound impertinent to someone who does not have any.

V.: Because common sense told me: "If you do not eat, you die." And of course both are important. So He smiled at that and said: "Yes, but Mine—my bread, will last forever, whereas yours does not last." He understood my humor and smiled and replied in that way.

J.N.: Do you have another anecdote?

V.: Another time, I was in church, a chapel rather, in Rhodes, Greece, in summer. It was horribly hot. It was the Vespers of the Blessed Virgin and, as you know, Orthodox chapels do not have seats, only a few for elderly people, and we stand. The Vespers seemed to last forever. They had been going on for more than two hours and I couldn't stand it any longer, because it was hot, and crowded, and I had a little group with me. I could no longer pay attention, they were repeating hymns of praise, and I was becoming distracted. My mind was elsewhere and at the same time, I was feeling quite guilty, and I was telling myself: "You have to show respect, you are in a chapel, it is Vespers, it is for the Blessed Virgin." But I couldn't stand it anymore; I couldn't help it. My eyes went to the profiles of the priests, one after the other, and there was a beard longer than the others, and I was counting all the beards to find out how many there were. I was bored to tears! And just at that moment I looked up and, as in every Orthodox Church or chapel, there is a representation of Christ-Pantocrator, Christ as He will appear on Judgment Day. That Christ-Pantocrator was incredibly beautiful. He is too often represented with a very stern look and strict features, as if ready to judge us; very impressive. But that one was very well done. He had a gentle look. And while I was looking up, I was seeing out of the corner of my eye Erwin, one of my friends, a young man who was converted when reading *True Life in God*. Since I was looking up he also looked up. What do I see? I see the Lord who is winking. A wink! My heart leaped with joy because Jesus was there. He was teasing me. I was standing and I was bored. He was saying: "Come on, just a little more, a little effort!" I was so happy I didn't say anything. I also thought that this was incredible. After ten minutes the service was over. We left. I get back into the car. Erwin comes to me and says into my ear so that nobody could hear, "Vassula, you know me. I am not hysterical, but when you looked up at the Christ-Pantocrator, I, too, looked at Him and He winked at me!" So he had seen Him also. It was a confirmation that it was really God.

J.N.: It's a very good anecdote. Do you have another one like it?

V.: Yes. I was in Israel. I had given meetings and had kept the last day for me, for some shopping in the old city. I wanted to window-shop for gifts for my family and friends. And I was quite pleased to be free, when a friend came to inform me that the Sisters of Bethlehem had prepared dinner for me in an hour's time and had arranged a meeting. My moment of freedom was then lost since I was returning to Switzerland the next day. So I looked up to Heaven with a gesture of the hands meaning, "Where can one find freedom?" And then I hear a voice saying: "In the Spirit." He said that so that I would witness to it.

J.N.: Something else?

V.: At one time, I was thinking about my angel's age and was trying to imagine what it meant to be two thousand, three thousand years old. It was an obviously preposterous idea and I finally burst into a nervous laugh, and apologized for that kind of absurd distraction. And my angel replied that I didn't have to apologize, because I had done it without malice.

J.N.: Could you quote a text from True Life in God *that would illustrate your loving and humorous relationship with God?*

V.: One day when God had called me I felt He was amused. He told me a little story, a parable, comparing me to a piece of driftwood.

I happened to be taking a walk nearby a river when I saw a drift-wood [God means me] drifting away with the worldly current; I leaned over and picked it out of the stream; I brought it Home with Me and planted it in My Garden of Delights; from a dry piece of wood I made out of you a Tree; I said: "grow! grow and take root in My Garden, in My own Property; and from your blossoms exhale a perfume to appease My Justice;" I said: "crops of fruit shall sprout each month and your leaves will be the cure to many;" now and then I amuse Myself in pruning you; My delight is to see flowers in blossom and a constant growth in your fruit alone, the Water from My Sanctuary can give you growth and Life; I, Yahweh, will see to it that you prosper; I take pleasure in picking now and then on My way pieces of driftwood; I can give life to anything I pick on My way; (November 13, 1991)

I would like to end this very dense chapter on the dialog between God and Vassula with a quotation from Father Fernando Umana's book, *Vassula, An Ecumenical Charism for Our Times*, because it gives a theologian's point of view.

In conclusion, we would like to establish the synthesis of what we believe to be the heart of God's message to the world through Vassula. We cannot find a more adequate word than "love." The entire message is an immense hymn of love from God to humankind and to each person in particular.

This love is evident and manifested in the very manner in which God speaks to Vassula. When He calls her "betrothed, bride, daughter, altar, city, seed, friend, beloved soul," many are surprised that she is called bride. When Vassula is questioned on that matter, she answers, "If God calls betrothed or bride the nuns who consecrate themselves to Him, why wouldn't He call a person that way who equally gives herself completely to God? If God has called 'bride' the people of Israel and the church, wouldn't He also refer the same way to every member of that church?" Moreover, especially during the first years of God's manifestation, the expression "I love you" occurs as often as the stipulation to always remain in union and united. For that reason, God often asks her, "Vassula, We, Us?" that is, always united. That "We, Us" is a way of reminding her that she must never feel alone or leave the Presence of Jesus. She must always be conscious of this Presence and remain intimate with Him, do everything in Him, with Him, by Him, and for Him.

Moreover, God showed her His infinitely merciful love by granting her abundant forgiveness for all her sins, drawing her out of the dreadful desert she was living in when she was waging war on God, entirely preoccupied with material things, without a single thought for Him whom she considered as a totally distant and remote being.

God had mercy on her littleness and her "nothingness" which, as He often reminds her, is precisely one of the reasons why He has called her for that mission.

On the other hand, the response God expected from her, as from each one of us, is a return of love: the offering of one's will, of one's freedom, daily renewed. God wants to hear this renewal of our complete self-surrender everyday. God complains on many occasions about the present state of mankind, saying to Vassula: "In them there is no love; love is missing; I thirst for love." God presents Himself to humanity as a beggar for love who knocks at every door and finds only rejection and indifference. If humanity despises Him now, it will later have to face Him as judge.

God does not ask much of men in order to give them His forgiveness, a look of repentance, a sigh of love, a smile, the shadow of a remorse for our bad conduct, to return to God; something that shows a desire for God, a thirst for Him, and immediately God will grant them His mercy and forgiveness.

CHAPTER TEN

The Mother of God

J.N.: I suggest that we talk about Mary. We have spoken little about her up to now. You have heard her, you see her?

V.: Yes. I see her but not often, because she mostly dictates. I hear her. The first time the Lord came with the Blessed Virgin, I was still in Bangladesh. He comes and tells me: "Look with whom I am. Tell Me with whom I am." I look, it was the Blessed Virgin. So I tell Him: "It's Your mother." Then He turns to me and says: "Your mother, too." Very simply, but still, right to the point. That answer is the truth; she is also our mother. It was to tell me, to tell everyone, to those who reject her, "Yes, she is your mother."

J.N.: When you see her, is it as a young girl, the young girl Mary of the Visitation, probably a sixteen-year-old? Or is it an older woman, the mother of Jesus at the foot of the cross? Which woman is she?

V.: There is an image that greatly impressed me. She was sitting on a white stone in a field. And I saw her back. She was bending like that, all dressed in black. It was a rather sad message. I was behind her and I walked toward her. She knew, of course, that I was approaching. She turned her face toward me to look at me and I saw a very pale face, beautiful, that of a young woman with very clear eyes, blue, full of tears. And she gave me the message she wanted to give me. At other times, but seldom, I see her as a young girl.

J.N.: As on the day she agreed to be the mother of God?

V.: Yes. That's it.

J.N.: Has she a marked eastern look?

V.: Not especially. I do not exactly know what you mean by eastern.

J.N.: I mean that the representation of her as given at Lourdes corresponds to the image of a French woman. Do you see her as the Virgin of Lourdes, as popular iconography represents her?

V.: I saw a pale face. And from what I see I cannot conclude whether she has a Jewish look or not. But I know that when I speak of the Lord, when I see the Lord, he has a Jewish face. I have seen faces similar to His when traveling in Israel. Often in Galilee, because Galileans have a clearer complexion and remarkable eyes. Their eyes are transparent like water, big and blue. And I told my traveling companions: "There, those are the eyes of Christ."

J.N.: Would you like to talk about the place Mary has in your piety?

V.: Yes. I would like to quote a few texts from *True Life in God*.

Do not ask: "how could it be that the Most High has assigned Her such a high throne in His Celestial Courts?" Look, not only have I assigned Her as the Queen of My Angels and My creatures but I have assigned Her to be My Throne. The Queen of heaven and earth is the Throne of the King of kings, for I, the Lord of All, have placed Her as first in My Sacred Heart. Born to be My Crown of Splendor, born to be the Vessel of the True Light who was made flesh from David's line, born to be My honor and My boast, the Spirit with Me and the Father said: "Mary full of grace, We are with you; We will hide none of the secrets from You; Our Breath will be your breath, pure emanation of Our Glory, Mary, Our image of Our Goodness, We give you Our Peace in Your Heart, in this perfect Heart I, the Son shall triumph; Our Heart will be Your Heart, a burning furnace of divine love, Our Soul will be

Your Soul, [soul should be understood as life, as in Luke 9:24] an august treasure, a Paradise for Us; Our Spirit will be Your Spirit. Yes, for anyone who is joined to Us is one spirit with Us." (March 25, 1996)

The Virgin Mary is the second Eve. This calls for an explanation. What had been lost and profaned by the first Eve had to be recovered. Through her acceptance of God's plan, through her obedience, Mary succeeded where Eve, through her disobedience had failed. Mary's obedience made possible the Incarnation of Jesus, consequently His sacrifice, and consequently redemption. Mary's obedience has therefore made it possible that, through the merits of redemption, heaven be opened not only for herself but also for all of us. In this way, thanks to the merits of Jesus, Mary has regained the paradise, lost by Eve for herself and all of us. This is why we are her children.

And it is also through Mary that the reign of Christ will return on earth. The reign of Christ on earth will be established in every heart through the outpouring of the Holy Spirit. The day will come when the arrogant crown of the powers of evil will be trampled upon by the Woman adorned with the sun, who is Mary, and by all her children. The Lord has given her enough power to conquer Satan and his whole empire; with her heel she will crush his head.

The idea entertained by certain persons that we consider Mary as a goddess is completely false. We love and honor Mary because she is our mother, before our earthly mother. We love her because she is the Mother of Jesus, our God. The Virgin Mary intercedes day and night with God for us, and God listens to her as He listened to her at Cana. I have received a message that speaks about Cana and also about those who reject Mary. This message, that I like very much, has been given to me by the Father:

Find your comfort in Her embrace and in those same arms that carried My Son through the desert into Egypt; honor the Mother who

95

honored Me with Her graciousness, why, have I not highly favored Her? I have done great things for the Woman clothed with the sun, so that from that day forward when My Spirit covered Her, all generations would call Her Blessed. Shame and dishonor are the lot who stopped honoring Her; I take no pleasure in your comments combined with sneers on the Woman so highly favored by Me and to each I will pay his due. Humble your spirit, humble it even more now and abstain from making faces when it comes to entreat Her intercession; who tells you that I shall not listen to Her? Has your Mother not interceded in Cana? These signs were performed so that your spirit may understand what your spirit rejects today (God is speaking only to those who reject our Blessed Mother and to those who do not give Her enough honor.); this sign was meant for all ages to come. The Woman adorned with the sun, adorned with My Holy Spirit, thrice Holy and who fills the world, ranks as Mother of God. (January 27, 1996)

Here is another passage about Mary dictated by her Son. The Lord begins by asking us what creature is like the heart of Mary. Since she is perfect, nobody is like her. And even in her grace she surpasses all the graces of God's angels. That passage amused me a lot because I was seeing the angels calling to each other about the Virgin Mary before Jesus had been conceived in her by the Holy Spirit. The Lord said:

This is why My Angels in throngs questioned one another: "who is this, behind Her veil?" "why are the crests of the mountains bowing down low, saluting Her, as She passes them by?" "who is this without a blemish in Her Heart and so pleasing to God?" "have you seen how all God's creation lowers its gaze as She passes by?" "who is She who is like a fountain that makes the gardens fertile by Her graces, this well of living water?" "who is She, with a Heart so pure with divine love, aspiring for God day and night, night and day, and in perfect union with the Most High?" "who is this Virgin who is so humble over Her great wealth of virtues and graces, that the supreme God's Eyes never leave Her?" many of My Angels remained silent in admiration, words had failed them…. (March 25, 1996)

CHAPTER ELEVEN

The End Times and the Apostasy of Christians

J.N.: You have often spoken of a sign that would appear in the sky. Could you explain what the "end of times" means to you?

V.: It is not the end of the world but the end of times; we are already in it. We are living in the end of times, and not the end of the world. The Blessed Virgin has promised, "At the end of times, I will raise apostles who will be called the apostles of the last days." And we see it today, with charismatic groups, testimonies, and the gifts of the Holy Spirit, who is giving profusely. Before, we had to merit a gift before receiving it. Now, even before we deserve it He gives a gift. We have all the signs of the end of times. Saint Paul says that we will recognize the end of times through two signs. The first is apostasy. The second is rebellion. And the signs are here today. We are seeing today, in the Catholic and Orthodox churches, a sort of rebellion, even very pronounced. The other sign of apostasy is there. A priest objected once that apostasy had always existed in the church.

J.N.: I was about to raise the same objection.

V.: Formerly, apostasy was an individual thing. Nowadays, it is general. It was never like today.

J.N.: So you believe that what is going on today is more serious than what happened in the past. For example, in the fourth or fifth century, there were more Arian heretics than Catholics, yet the Arians have completely disappeared. In the Middle Ages, from 1409 to 1414, there were up to three popes at the same time. There was the Reformation and, in response to it, this form of apostasy we call the wars of religion. That makes a lot of apostasies in the course of history.

V.: But what the Lord considers as serious, and which perhaps we do not understand, is that the prophecies of Daniel are being accomplished. In chapter twenty-four of the Gospel of Matthew, the Lord says that at the end of times, Daniel's prophecy will be fulfilled. He says that the perpetual sacrifice will be abolished and the abomination of desolation established in the sanctuary. The perpetual sacrifice is the Eucharist. But it is not only Communion in itself. Why is the Eucharist being questioned? Because it proves the divinity of Christ and the Resurrection. And this is what the enemy wishes to remove completely, that which is the life of the church. For God it may be more important than we think.

J.N.: So, for you, apostasy is made up of the theses of certain theologians, according to whom there is no such thing as the divinity of Jesus or further, that the Presence in the Eucharist is not real but purely symbolic. In your opinion, these are two elements of the apostasy.

V.: Apostasy concerns those to whom divine truth has been given and who have denied this divine truth. They are the apostates. It does not concern those who were born Muslim, for example, and who have never received this truth. I mean that apostasy concerns those to whom the entire truth has been given, that is, the divinity of Christ, His Presence in the Eucharist. They are the Orthodox and the Catholics.

J.N.: So a theologian who denies these two truths is an apostate?

V.: If he is Catholic.

J.N.: But there are Reformed Churches, in this canton for example, who consider that when pastors celebrate the Lord's Supper they do it only to commemorate the Last Supper celebrated by Jesus. For them, there is no real presence of Christ under the species of the bread and wine.

V.: They deny nothing of what has been given to them through their particular tradition and they can't be blamed. No more than a Buddhist.

J.N.: But the ancestors of the Reformed have known those truths at a certain time in their history.

V.: In the past. We are talking of today.

J.N.: Surely in view of this world that has apostatized, as you say, Heaven must do something. It is obviously a pessimistic vision of the close of this century. Your pessimistic vision, or God's negative judgment on this century, has a number of reasons to draw on. You have spoken of the apostasy of many Christians, of the desertion of many religious, men and women, of the legalization of abortion. But there is also, as in every century, a message of hope in the story, some positive elements.

V.: Everything is happening as if we were going through the pains of childbirth now. Immediately after, there will be joy because of the newborn child and the pains will be forgotten. We are now going through this time of pains. The pain of the Mystical Body, which is the Church, can really be seen in the present persecution. But in all the messages I receive God always leaves hope. God is not a God that will morally destroy us and then crush us. God always elevates the soul. Even when He reprimands, He reprimands in such a way that in the end He encourages, "But come! I forgive you in any case, as long as you admit your sin."

But afterward there will be joy. And what is joy? It is the unity of the Church and then, something more, a radical transformation of the whole earth, because there will be like a second Pentecost, according to the prayer of [Pope] John XXIII. And it is coming. While the evil is growing—with the persecution of the Church, the perpetual misunderstandings within the Church, and in families also—God is not just standing there with arms folded; He is acting. He does beautiful things at the same time. Something is happening under the impulse of the Holy Spirit, which is beginning to be poured out on us.

J.N.: I would like to suggest perhaps some astonishing things in recent history. I would like to emphasize certain positive changes in society since the beginning of the Industrial Revolution. For example, the death penalty has been abolished. Torture is forbidden. Social security is such that people do not fall into desperate circumstances; they receive unemployment insurance, they get medical treatment, they receive a pension in their old age. Free and compulsory education makes it possible for all children to go to school. Women, who used to be considered second-class citizens, now have equal rights with men. Don't you find that when looking at the city we are in, the country we are in, the continent we are on, men have every reason to be pleased with what has been accomplished during the past two or three centuries? That does not mean, of course, that we are living in a perfect society, far from it, but that we have taken a few steps in the right direction.

V.: All that is very fine. But we cannot mock God. All that has been done in the field of social security is very good. But something is missing from within this organization; it is religion. It is as if these reformers wanted to take God's place, to decide everything. Ezekiel 28 explains that, "You think you are God, you sit on the throne of God and you play at being God." And He gave me a message about that. He does not deny charity, but it is not enough. We must understand that we are not God. We cannot legalize abortion because it is against the Ten Commandments. And we want to play God and decide what is right and what is wrong. And it's like the first fall. The serpent came to tempt Eve, to have her eat the fruit from the forbidden tree, telling her that she would be able to know good from evil, and that she would be like God. Today we are repeating that story. We take upon ourselves the role of God and we decide what must be done, what is right and what is not right. I'm thinking especially about abortion.

J.N.: That's negative. You do not mention anything positive. You certainly know the text from St. Paul where he says: "If I have all the faith and all the hope in the world but have not love, it is of no use to me." But he has not said the opposite. That is, if you have charity, but not faith and hope, you are missing the essential.

V.: At every page, St. Paul talks about the Risen Christ. Certainly God will judge us at the end according to the measure of love we have had on earth. But, at the same time, I cannot accept the vision that we live in an ideal world. You have pointed out examples of progress, and I agree that we have made progress. But we have lost something essential and that is religion. The whole truth is that God is Trinity and Love.

J.N.: We both know, you and I, some atheists who are quite worthy from a human point of view, because very often they dedicate themselves to a cause and some of them sacrifice their life. So, in your opinion, while we may greatly admire what they do something is missing?

V.: Yes. Especially nowadays. In the days of our grandmothers, there was much more religion. The Bible was read in the home.

101

People were closer to God. Now, we start by forgetting God and then we play God. What's missing today is religion, truth.

J.N.: You consider that these atheists—who are benefactors, who volunteer for certain causes—if they do not have faith it is because, at a certain moment, they were offered faith and they clearly refused it.

V.: In that case they are apostates, not atheists. Atheists were born into a family that was already atheistic. For example, the Bushmen of the Kalahari are atheists. They grew up in the bush. But God will not blame them, because they know nothing. They are like that. It's like a garden full of flowers, and many different flowers. So, He will not blame them. Since they grew up in the bush they do not know Him. He will judge them on their love perhaps. But the apostate will have to give an accounting before God, because he was given the truth and nonetheless rejected it.

J.N.: In our society some children are born into families where they never hear about religion. Those children are not apostates. They are natural atheists who grow up in complete indifference.

V.: My children were growing in such an atmosphere before my conversion. As soon as I was converted I asked my son: "And Easter, do you know what Easter is?" He looked at me and said, "Yes, of course. The school is closed. It's the holidays." That's all he knew about Easter.

J.N.: In this society where religious practice is apparently poor, a sociological survey was made by a professor of the theological faculty of the University of Lausanne. This survey asked questions about religion and religious practice. We found, and it was no surprise, that ten percent of the people attend church regularly in the society we live in. But we found that many people, who were not churchgoers, believed in God, believed in Jesus, believed in the Resurrection and that quite an astonishing percentage, about fifty percent of the people, pray every day. Does that surprise you?

V.: I am surprised, yes. They pray just the same? Fifty percent of them?

J.N.: They pray. And it's not that they pray rarely, they pray every day. We sort of feel that we live in a society where religious practice is poor because people do not find in churches what they should find, but they are looking for it through direct contact with God.

V.: My parents were living like that. My father is now deceased. He went to church from time to time, but every Sunday he practiced his religion at home. My mother, even today, talks a lot about God at home. She has faith and prays a lot, but always at home.

J.N.: Do you think that the churches, as they are presently, the many Christian Churches, are failing in their pastoral duty; that is, they do not do what they should so that people practice?

V.: The massive apostasy is a sign that something is wrong. Otherwise the churches would be full. Now they are not. When they are full, the young people are not there. This young generation is already beginning to be atheistic. And they no longer find God. They often tell me that they are not interested in going to church to listen to priests because it has no effect on them. On the other hand, there are pastors and priests who do give us God. When I was in church last week, the priest gave a very beautiful homily. He explained the Gospel and gave advice for our lives, which was very clear, precise, and transparent. It really made us think. When it was over I told him, because he was going by me, "I liked your homily very much." He was so happy. "Is it true?" We have to encourage those priests who work hard, because there is a lot of discouragement, many priests who have lost the desire to work, to dedicate themselves. They wonder if it's doing any good. If a celebration or a teaching has moved us, we must encourage them and thank them. We criticize priests a lot, but we do not encourage them enough.

J.N.: It seems that you have heard many homilies that brought you in the end very little, that put you off or bored you. In your opinion why are those homilies not up to what they should be?

V.: The action of the Holy Spirit is missing. The messages on the action of the Holy Spirit say: "The inner power and strength of My Church is My Holy Spirit who sets you on fire to witness with ardor and zeal. And thus He becomes the flavor of your homilies." I think that if a homily is dull, it comes from the human mind and certainly not from the Holy Spirit. As soon as we try to communicate a message from the Holy Spirit He touches the soul, for it knows that it is not a man but the Holy Spirit who is talking.

J.N.: This is a beautiful comment on homilies. Would you have a similar comment on liturgy? As a rule do the songs and prayers, as perceived by the faithful in Masses or Protestant services, help Christians? People are often bored during celebrations and stop attending them.

V.: That depends on the priest. People are a little like horses, very sensitive. They know right away what is going on. If a priest says his mass through obligation, people feel it right away. But if he does it because he loves God, if he does it with his heart and believes in it, we feel it right away. His faith is immediately communicated to the souls. We can find both situations presently; we must not generalize. But I often repeat that if priests are really in this serious state of apparent lack of faith, the lay people must pray for them. With much praying they can change in the end. Whereas criticizing them and nothing else, discourages them even more and they quit completely.

J.N.: Do you think that, in certain Masses, the priest is not convinced of the real Presence of Jesus in the Eucharist?

V.: Yes, there are those serious cases of priests who have lost faith. A bishop in the United States told me that he had caught one of his priests emptying what was left in the chalice in the washbasin. But we must not generalize or criticize gratuitously. There are apostates everywhere, even among priests, but not especially among them.

J.N.: Whatever the magnitude of the apostasy, is this end of times, which you tirelessly proclaim a sign for hastening conversion?

V.: It is indeed. Now is the time of mercy. The Lord announces that we must hasten to convert because this time will not last. It is a time during which God's merciful calls to conversion abound. After this time there will be silence. There will be no more calls. It will be too late.

J.N.: Therefore a kind of dark night for all humanity? Can the end of times be one of those cataclysms that you mention? You allude to the image of the earth's gravitation that would be altered?

V.: It could be only symbolic and I hope it is. But I am convinced that the fire the messages talk about is not only symbolic.

J.N.: If this conversion, asked for with such insistence, should happen in our times, would it delay or suppress the end of times, in the sense of the dialog between Abraham and Yahweh concerning the destruction of Sodom and Gomorrah? Would fifty righteous persons be enough, or thirty?

V.: Yes, I agree with that interpretation. It might be simpler here to quote a message.

I will deprive no one from My Light; no one should remain imprisoned in darkness. My Father is afflicted by untimely grieving and the

retribution He has reserved for this faithless and apostatized generation is at their very doors now; I shall send in the chaos they are living
in, the Vessel (Our Blessed Mother), who carried Me in flesh to carry
this time again My Word, so that I come to them like a drop of morning dew in their desert; I will send My Mother to teach them little by
little My ways and correct those who offend Me; why, I Myself, shall
descend too in this desert to enliven the dead; Instruction and Wisdom
shall be given freely to them. We shall come with Our Heart in Our
Hand and offer it to them; and like Two Lamps, standing side by side,
We will shine on them. I will not be slow in executing My Plan and a
time of Mercy will be granted to them all; this is why, I will raise disciples in these end of times to build what lies now in ruin; I shall send
them to witness in My Name; I shall send them where shrubs bear fruit
that never ripens and where the path of True Knowledge is neglected.
My precious ones [the prophets](Those selected and sent out to testify
and prophesy), will be sent in the entrails of this earth, where sin is
coiled up as a serpent in its nest, to extirpate and uproot evil; I shall
send those ones to uproot the great Plan of the Beast; I shall grant
them in their special mission the power and their actions will be crowned
with success; with My Holy Spirit they will withstand fearsome devils;
with courage and perseverance they will pay no heed to the stoning
they will receive; My Holy Spirit will be their guide and companion,
guiding them prudently in their undertakings; I will execute My promise without delay and dispatch My Holy Spirit from the Heavens to
work with them and teach them all that I have already given them; I
shall open their mouth and fill it with My Word, and their tongue will
be like a sword; I will guard My precious ones closely from My enemies
[The apostates, followers of the Beast.): the oppressors, in those days. I
will save them from the traps set for them and from the fatal hard stone
aimed on them; no, My all-powerful Hand will not lack means of saving them; I will treat this generation leniently in spite of its wickedness.
(January 19, 1995)

J.N.: Would this chastisement, if it comes, be coming from
God?

V.: It is we who are calling the chastisement upon ourselves.
God does not like to chastise. But we provoke God's justice, because we must not forget that He is a God of love, of mercy, but

also of justice. The end of times does not mean the end of the world; it's the end of an era in which Satan was given freedom to tempt us. In this end of times, Christ unseals for us, reveals to us in the Scriptures the prophecies of Daniel, because they are coming about now. But He is also unsealing many chapters of the Book of the Apocalypse. There is a concordance between the books of the prophets Daniel and Ezekiel and the Book of the Apocalypse. The beast (which the prophet) Daniel speaks about— the Beast which is the enemy—and which we find also in chapter 13 of the Apocalypse, represents today, in large measure, the apostates and rebels who plan to ruin the Church of Christ, and above all to abolish the Eucharist and present Christ only as a prophet, a sage. Christ told me once that His kingdom on earth is the Church and the Eucharist is the life of the Church. By no longer acknowledging that He is the Second Person of the Holy Trinity, these apostates persecute the divinity of Christ. They deny that He is God's only son and God Himself, and they deny His resurrection, considering it as merely symbolic. Christ tells us that in this end of times, rebellion is already at work, but secretly, and that he who is holding it back must first be removed before the rebel shows himself in the open. And He tells us that he who holds back the rebellion is the pope. Christ tells us to remain firm and keep the traditions that we have been taught. He warns us that the Church will go through a terrible trial, such as it has never known before. Many times He tells us that if someone crosses our path bringing a doctrine different from the one He has Himself established, we must not listen to him because such people come from the deceiver.

Christ comes to our aid to warn us of these dangers. He tells us that rationalism and materialism are the fundamental enemies of His Church, because they both lead to atheism. In this end of times, God reveals to us sad things that are happening in the

Church, but He also reveals good things full of hope. The good news is that His Church will be renewed by His Holy Spirit of Truth, who renews and revives. By His Mercy, we are experiencing a time of grace. In this end of times—which we are living today and which are times of darkness—where apostasy is growing daily as well as rebellion, there is also the dawn of light, that of the Holy Spirit. Today, in many places, God sends us the Blessed Virgin who is appearing to teach us how to pray, to remind us of the divine laws, to bring us back to God.

CHAPTER TWELVE

Heaven and Hell

J.N.: You have already mentioned hell, purgatory, and heaven. Could you say a few words about heaven? Have you had a vision of heaven?

V.: I have had symbolic visions. We can't say that it is a description of heaven as it actually is. It's not that at all. The Lord gives me what He wants to show me at that time. He told me, "You shall be My visitor in heaven. Come, I will show you." So, right away He takes me in spirit and it is the Father. So I find myself somewhere, in a very beautiful garden. There was a fantastic light, but no sun. And it was only light. It was like a beautiful garden. I knew that the Father was beside me. He takes my hand. He does not let me turn my head to look at Him. That was out of the question. Still, I longed to. But I couldn't turn my head. It was like that. And He tells me, "Look. Look at the hemisphere. What can you see over there? Tell Me!" Then I look and I see like a sun, a ball of light. Then He tells me, "Come, let us go toward this light. It is My Abode." He led me. It is a light, like a heart if you will, a circle. And then we get ready to enter this abode. He tells me, "This abode is very, very holy. Look, what can you see around that light." And then I was seeing like spots moving around it, but I couldn't make out anything, and then I look again and I see billions of angels encircling this abode, all sorts of angels. And then I enter into the light and when I enter, I was expecting to see a really blinding light. It was not that at all. I see blue, it was all blue inside and round, and the wall was not a wall; they were archangels, tall, one stuck to the other, one on top of another, stuck all together forming a dome.

J.N.: A cupola?

V.: A cupola. But all made up of archangels. Much later I learned that the color blue, in icons, represents God's divinity. The symbolic blue. Then He tells me, "Look up!" I look and the cupola opens up like a flower, and I see a battle. Like in the old days, with horses charging, I see a battle and He says to me, "That is the battle going on right now on earth." In a mystical way if you will. "The fallen angels with Satan are fighting against St. Michael and his angels, and you also, you are standing in the midst of this battle. This battle has begun to divide the good from the bad among men." After that He tells me, "Look at that one in the middle." Then I see an angel, but not like the others, because it was as if a light was coming out of him that was not blue like the light of the other angels. He was dressed in a sparkling white robe, he had golden hair, and he held in His hand a beautiful gold sword. He tells me: "You see? This is My Word. It cuts and pierces; the sword represents My Word." And the vision vanished immediately. Another time I had a different vision. He tells me: "Come and see My House where you will all go." Have you seen the Milan Cathedral?

J.N.: Yes, of course.

V.: It was almost the same thing. When I enter this cathedral I see almost the same thing, thick columns, one after the other, but not quite on the side. The only difference was that, instead of the cathedral wall it was like balconies with rooms. It was where we were to live. But in the middle, from one end to the other along the length of the nave, there was a long table, and there was not one centimeter free. It was full. And he said, "That is for all of you." And I heard something on the side, on my right, I remember; I looked and I saw a fountain. This fountain was alive almost. It was like water, but alive. And it was silvery, it was gushing forth. It was so beautiful and I said, "This water is alive." I go this way and He lets me go into a room. As I go in, there is like a balcony; I look through and at first what I felt was not only nature, it was peace, a peace such as I have never felt on earth, an extraordinary peace which does not yet exist on earth, and I told myself, "If only I would die, I could be there always, in this room where I was seeing this nature." That's all.

J.N.: Do you pray sometimes to go to heaven instantly and not come back to earth?

V.: Yes. The Lord has even put that question to me many times. To live as I live is suffering. I have to be like everybody, although I am not. Deep down in my heart I am different…even if I look like everybody else outwardly. One cannot hide behind a veil. I love my family. He gave me a family. Here, I have to do my duty as a mother, but it is painful. Everything external is painful to me. It is as if it hurts. All that I used to like has become painful. When my husband asks me to go to the swimming pool with him, I can't. It's pure suffering. I really refuse to go to the pool. But at home, to take part in the life of the home, if he wants to look at a movie that doesn't interest me, I look at it with him; otherwise we would no longer have a life together. To remain on this earth is painful.

J.N.: Could you quote a text from True Life in God *that would explain heaven?*

V.: The best description is perhaps the message of November 22, 1986.

What can you see daughter? Can you see what I have for you in My Hall? A table that is full, full of blessings, abundant and with all the fruits of My garden. I prepared it and laid it out for My children…daughter, what can you see now? Can you see My fountain?

Yes! this sparkling water is for you to drink. It is living water. Feel the surroundings of My House; yes! It is big and there is space for many. I have rooms for all of you. My House is Holy; My House is Peace. Come now and see; tell Me how you feel; do you feel happy? Yes! There is love and peace. I am present; you can feel My Presence; I am Peace. Daughter, now that you have seen the splendor of My House, go and tell them, go and proclaim to My children My glorious Name. Bring them this message of peace, tell them of My table, which is laid out for them and of the space My House has to offer and that I, Yahweh, am waiting for them. Let them come to Me so that they share My glory. Daughter, you have done well, I will progress you. I, God, love you; go in peace and love all your duties, beloved.

What struck me most, in that vision which I had in my mind, was the sensation of tranquility I felt while looking from the veranda at that peaceful panorama. All sadness, all cares had suddenly vanished. I only felt an incredible peace. In fact, in one of His messages, God reminded me that in paradise there is no more sadness. He said, "Tears will dry out, sorrows will leave you, sufferings will vanish, despondency will end." On the other hand, I would like to add that we should not think that the whole of paradise is limited to this one vision. All the visions given to me are only to represent and explain a particular message. Like all intellectual visions, they are only given to enrich an explanation in the Scriptures or in the Tradition.

J.N.: Let's talk about purgatory. You mention purgatory.

V.: This is interesting because, in our Orthodox Church we do not talk about purgatory. I was never taught that. However, at the very beginning, when I was still with my angel, God let a few souls from purgatory approach me. Long before that, I was about nineteen, long before the call; here in Switzerland I would see, from time to time, with the eyes of the heart, many souls. They were all alike, the same color, ash-gray. And I couldn't distinguish men from women. But I knew that there were men and women.

And they came all around me. I never was afraid of them because they looked peaceful. They all sat on the floor. They were talking to each other about me, "Hush! Do not disturb her!" I became used to them. And then, when I was seeing them like that, I would say to myself, "Ah! Always the dead!" Because I didn't know how to say "souls," I would say: "There's the dead again!" But it never frightened me. Much later, Jesus explained to me that those souls were waiting for my prayers, my sacrifices, fasting, penance, everything so that they would be delivered, and that I would see them in heaven one day. So, one day, in the beginning with my angel, he had me meet a few souls to speak to me. Then one soul comes to me and says, "Give me a blessing and pray for me." I said, "Why does she want a blessing from me?" Then I said, "But I don't know how." She says, "Pray for me!" "Which prayer? I don't know how to pray." And she gives me a short prayer, which I have since forgotten. She gave it to me orally. She said: "Repeat that for me!" And I repeated it. She was quite happy and was gone. It seemed to me that she was going up. And then she disappeared and other souls came, all fervent, in a group, asking me this: "Go to the church and get holy water! We'll tell you why." I go. I ask the priest for holy water and he gives me a little bottle. I get back home. They tell me, "Now, sprinkle us!" I say, "But how can I sprinkle you since I do not see you." I could see the water concretely there, physically, whereas I saw those souls inwardly. How was I to sprinkle them? That didn't make any sense. The souls said to me: "Put water in the hollow of your hand, close your eyes with the intention of sprinkling us, and sprinkle!" And I did it. Oh! It was as if the entire purgatory was coming to me for that little drop of water. It was so refreshing to the soul; they were all happy.

J.N.: You describe a contact with souls from purgatory. The place itself, have you ever visited it?

V.: I saw myself in purgatory. The Lord told me, "Would you like to see where your soul would have been before I came to get you?" Then He gave me a vision and I saw myself. The sky was dark. There was no light, not even gray, dark as now. And it was like a desert. No garden. It was dry! And I saw a baby. A baby lying on the floor. And it was I. I saw myself as a baby on the floor. And so I was seeing myself. And the eyes were yellowish like those of a sick person. No strength. So sick spiritually that I couldn't stand up. My breath was like asthma; I could barely breathe. And I feel a presence approaching, but I couldn't see the head. I only felt the presence of a good being. My hand, which didn't have any strength, was clinging to His sleeve. I didn't want to let go because I knew He was my Savior. And when my hand gripped Him, He was so moved, the Savior. He took me and brought me back where I should have been. But it was awful, the place I saw.

J.N.: As you say, the Orthodox Church does not mention purgatory. It is an idea that appeared in the Catholic West in the tenth century. It was not mentioned before.

V.: Yes, it's true. And then, what I noticed later, when I was in Romania not long ago, were the icons that represented the soul of the Virgin; only the soul, and it was like a baby. And on all the drawings that the angel did for me, because he was making drawings for me, he represented me as a soul, as a baby. We are like babies if you will. All souls.

J.N.: Let's talk about hell.

V.: The Lord made me have a look at hell so that I could bear witness that hell exists and refute those who do not believe in hell. Satan is an evil spirit who exists, not an abstract concept. All of a sudden I find myself in a grotto. The earth was dark gray, very fine sand, as if volcanic. And it was slimy on the ground. Of course the Lord cannot descend into hell. But, since a vision is not real, He was in the vision and said to me, "Look!" And I see Satan standing in front of me. He had his back to me. Satan can transform himself into a beast, a dog, into the Blessed Virgin, anything. But this time I saw Satan as a man. A person. Black hair. A rather ugly person at that. And he had lava in his hand, a flowing fire. And he was throwing lava on the heads of the people. He was continuously burning them. There were screams inside that grotto. Much further I heard, like an echo, the roar of burning fire. When I came a little nearer Satan felt that I was looking at him. He turns around and sees me. He looks me in the eye and spits on the floor and with disgust says, "We even have worms nowadays, coming to bother me." He is yelling like a mad man, totally mad. He yells. He says with hatred, "You will all come here with me!" And then, in my mind only, I say to myself, "That's what he thinks." He read my thought. With hatred, he said to me, "Since you thought that, you'll see, I'll torture the souls even more." And he was going to throw more lava, when the Lord paralyzed his hand.

J.N.: When you were speaking about heaven, just now, God said to you, "I have rooms for all of you." That seems to contradict the fact that there are souls in hell or in purgatory.

V.: That is to say heaven is our home; we have to live there. God prepared this home for us. But in other messages He says, with great sorrow, "I do not want to see a room empty for eternity." That is the room that had been prepared for them, whereas they were, instead falling down into hell.

J.N.: Would that mean, as certain theologians would say, that hell does exist, but that it is empty, or that it will be emptied in the end?

V.: Only God knows the answer. As for me, I am neither God nor a theologian.

J.N.: Could you quote another text from True Life in God *on the same subject?*

V.: Yes. Here is a message that is a good summation of heaven and hell.

come let us leave; I want you to write all this down, I will edit for you. Be near Me, beloved. I want My children to understand that their souls live and that evil exists. All what is written in My Blessed Word is not a myth; Satan exists and seeks to ruin your souls. (March 7, 1987)

when My angels who had been given supreme authority rebelled against Me and destruction took the best out of them, My Justice did not spare them, they were thrown down to the underworld to wait for the day of Judgment; they too will be judged before the very eyes of everyone, and ah! … what a terrible sight that will be! I will judge every-one according to what he has done and not done; in front of My Throne everyone will stand in silence and in awe for the Day of this final Judgment will be so dreadful that it will make everyone tremble with fright in front of the Supreme Judge that I Am;

You will all see a huge number of fallen angels who were driven out of heaven and fought in bitterness and spite Michael the archangel and his angels; yes, your eyes will see My Rivals, the Rivals of the Holy One, of the Anointed One; you will all see those fallen angels, adepts of Lucifer, the primeval serpent who tried to lead My sons and My daughters all astray. You will see multitudes of those who defiled My Name and transgressed My Law, those who refused to be reared and fostered by My Holiness and preferred to be labeled on their forehead by the Deceiver…(I was here given a vision of this multitude of fallen angels standing in front of God's Throne in the Day of Judgment. It was awesome, and sad.) (July 20, 1992)

Yes, Vassula, a harsh vision has been shown you; I tell you: I will soon come with My saints to pronounce judgment on the world and to sentence the guilty;

Today My Grace is being revealed to all mankind to renew you all with My Holy Spirit before My Day and remind you of My Law. I will in that Day repay everyone according to what he deserves; I have said that I will severely punish anyone who insults the Spirit of Grace and treats My Spirit as foolish; that is why you should stay awake. (July 20, 1992)

CHAPTER THIRTEEN

That All Be One

One of the strong points of Vassula's message concerns Christian unity. While continuing to practice her faith within the Greek Orthodox Church into which she had been baptized, Vassula also takes part in Catholic celebrations when during her travels she does not find an Orthodox Church. She is also speaking to Christians of all denominations. This is not without causing reactions ranging from amazement to opposition. Let's simply recall a passage from the Notification published by *L'Osservatore Romano*.

Moreover, by habitually sharing in the sacraments of the Catholic Church, even though she is Greek Orthodox, Mrs. Ryden is causing considerable surprise in various circles of the Catholic Church. She appears to be putting herself above all ecclesiastical jurisdiction and every canonical norm, and in effect, is creating an ecumenical disorder that irritates many authorities, ministers, and faithful of her own church, as she puts herself outside the ecclesiastical discipline of the latter.

The Memorandum for prudent pastoral behavior issued by the diocese of Sion, Switzerland and published on September 1, 1991, also includes a critical passage of Vassula's attitude.

Vassula Ryden is not Catholic and her initiatives do not answer to an official ecumenical dialog.... The "ecumenical" behavior of Vassula Ryden is too ambiguous. Now, within and in spite of the difficulties and hopes of ecumenism, all the denominations that are partners in dialog loyally desire to affirm what they confess. Confusion will not help the progress of unity. For the time being, every Christian belongs necessarily to a specific church.

The situation is well summed up in a retort, almost a quip, by Monsignor. Mamie when he was Bishop of Fribourg, "What's terrible about that woman is that she's trying to be simultaneously Orthodox and Catholic." This anecdote is told by Father Francis Frost of the Ecumenical Institute of Geneva. Apocryphal or not, it is a good illustration of the mixed feelings raised by Christians who feel that they are Christians first before belonging "necessarily" to a specific denomination. Vassula is at the source of a very obvious "ecumenical disorder" about which I asked her opinion.

J.N.: What does the pope's primacy mean to you? There are many ways to look at it. According to the point of view of the World Council of Churches it is a primacy of honor given to the Bishop of Rome in memory of St. Peter, which does not entail any particular right in matters related to the definition of doctrine or discipline within the churches. Does the role of the pope mean, for you, something more than this primacy of honor?

V.: In the messages, Christ calls him the Vicar of His Church. When I am addressing Roman Catholic circles, I give the messages as received from the Lord. He tells them to obey the pope blindly. We must obey him because disobedience does not come from God; it comes from Satan. Since I am Orthodox, this position surprises some people who ask me why I have not converted to Roman Catholicism. These persons do not listen to and do not read the pope's encyclicals that never asked that the Orthodox become Roman Catholic. He calls the Orthodox Churches sister churches. "Come and unite with us because the body cannot breathe with one lung only; it needs both lungs."

J.N.: It is one of John Paul II's favorite sentences.

V.: And so I say, "Follow what the pope says!" As for myself, I follow what the pope and the Ecumenical Patriarch Bartholomew I tell us. And the Lord talks the same way as the pope. He says:

"Both hands of the body have to join as in prayer." And the body works with both hands. It cannot work with one hand and forget the other.

J.N.: So, if this unity were to come about, it would not be a union where the Orthodox, Anglican, Lutheran churches, that are the closest to the Catholics, would submit to Rome. They would keep their structure, they would keep their liturgy, but they would consider themselves in union with Rome.

V.:   I can answer for the Eastern Church that is the sister church to the Roman Catholic Church. The other churches are deprived of the holy sacraments. In the messages, Christ brings up the fact that the Eucharist is the basis of the life of His Church. If His Church lacks luster, He says, it is because many churches have abolished the perpetual sacrifice. The Lord says first of all: "It is unity in the heart." It is not so much an external movement as an interior process. And by this He means, "In your conversion, you will unite. In conversion, you will blossom in unity." It is a movement that goes deeper in the heart than in institutions. As long as Christians will not convert and do not love Christ, no union is possible. I was recently invited, in Stockholm, by Pastor [Hans] Lundberg who welcomed me to St. Catherine's Church. He told me this, which made a great impression on me: "We have made a great mistake in minimizing the place of the Blessed Virgin. She has an immeasurable role to play and it is only now that I realize it." I enter his church and I discover a statue of the Blessed Virgin in front of where I was to speak. The church was full of Lutherans and Catholics. I gave my testimony. And after the testimony, he came, quite moved, and presented me with a gift, in front of everybody, a statue of the Blessed Virgin carrying the Baby Jesus. It really impressed me. And I asked how such a change in attitude could have happened with Lutherans who are very strict regarding the Virgin and statues. Someone in the assembly answered that it came from the faithful themselves; they feel such a need, they want unity. They find that through the messages of *True Life in God* there is hope.

J.N.: Are there also in Switzerland, Protestants who attend your meetings?

V.: Absolutely. There are Protestants who take Communion in the Roman Catholic or Orthodox churches because they believe in the true real Presence of Christ in the Eucharist; there are Protestants who practice the sacrament of confession.

J.N.: Some priests have told me that. We may naturally ask the question: "Where is the ultimate obstacle if the faithful of the different denominations have such a thirst for unity and overlook all the disputes that have existed in the past?"

V.: The lay people have no problem with uniting. The Lord gave me a vision of three iron bars. To unite, the heads have to bend. He was really speaking of the heads. They must learn to bend.

J.N.: You are quite clear on that subject. However, we get the impression from your vision or in the message that the Orthodox and Reformed churches will return to a common trunk that would be the Catholic Church. Is that the way you see things?

V.: It's not two bars bending toward the third, but rather three bars bending in the same direction. To bend signifies union in humility and love. The Lord told me that many among those who are working for Christian unity are rigid and stiff as iron bars.

J.N.: The message seems to say that the three churches are equally holy and equally sinners?

V.: I cannot answer you because He did not speak to me in those terms.

120

J.N.: You have, of course, no precise idea on the sequence of events or on a date. You are persuaded that union will take place, but you cannot say when or how?

V.: No, none of the messages gives this kind of precision. I, too, would like very much to know. But I know it's quite near.

J.N.: You said the other day that the message insists that the lay people feel more and more responsible for the church.

V.: The lay people do a lot now for the church. We see it in the meetings they organize. I know groups of lay people who fast twice a week, every Wednesday and Friday; many do sacrifices; many pray constantly for priests, for the church.

J.N.: To avoid getting everything mixed up, let's make a distinction between what, on the one hand, we call the original Church, that is, the assembly of the faithful and, on the other hand, what is commonly called the church today, that is, the ecclesiastical structure, the clergy, the bishops, the different parts of the church, the officials, if you will. We must not play with words and forget the difference between the two. Do the laity, the church members, the ordinary believers really need this ecclesiastical apparatus? Does it help them or, on the contrary, does it weigh on them?

V.: In every community there must be a leader who controls things. Otherwise there would be chaos; we wouldn't have a church, but sects. The church will always have bishops—leaders, if you will, to control. But we, the lay people, are also indispensable to the church. We are part of the church. Christ left us one Church, but He had barely left us to return to Heaven, when this Church divided. Division is a sin. In my church, certain monks sometimes give the impression of claiming a monopoly on God and handing out God to the faithful parsimoniously. Any Christian may obtain direct contact with God through prayer and purification.

J.N.: In your opinion, all Christians are equal. There are no first or second-class Christians—chiefs and subordinates.

V.: Certainly, but the laity cannot say mass or hear confession, and they must obey their bishop. They cannot disobey simply because they feel like it. We have to obey even if it is difficult. Except that we cannot obey a bishop who rebels against the pope or against Tradition. To whom are we to listen, the pope or this bishop? We must listen to the pope.

J.N.: In the case of an unworthy pope, for example, Alexander VI from the Borgia family who reigned at the end of the fifteenth century, are we obliged to obey him?

V.: But the present pope is not unworthy.

J.N.: Certainly not. There is no comparison possible between John Paul II and Alexander Borgia.

V.: If there is no comparison possible, since we are living today and not in the Renaissance, I answer simply that we must obey the present pope.

J.N.: What are your relations with the World Council of Churches in Geneva? Have you been invited or have you asked to be invited?

V.: No. I was invited. They had heard about me. Little by little *True Life in God* circulated all over the place. Reverend Emilio Castro, a former Catholic from Uruguay, who had become Methodist, invited me after talking to Father Bria, a Romanian Orthodox priest, and Mr. Todor Sabev, a lay theologian. Reverend Emilio Castro asked to meet me before the appointed meeting. He believes in the reality of private revelations. In his opinion, Jesus manifests Himself when the Church needs Him, as was the case with St. Teresa of Avila.

J.N.: Did many people come to hear you?

V.: Perhaps more in quality than in quantity. There were at least thirty-five people from the offices of the World Council of Churches itself who had come to hear me.

J.N.: First you gave a talk, then they asked questions?

V.: I proposed to take only excerpts from *True Life in God* that speak of unity and to read them directly, because it is not I who speak. I asked the Lord what to select. I prayed a lot. I said that we must choose only a few passages because I didn't have much time, only half an hour. So the Lord chose the strongest excerpts. It is, of course, quite trying to find oneself before an assembly of theologians who can set all kinds of traps for you. But when I read what the Lord gives me, I feel within me such strength and confidence that no one could contradict me, not even on the slightest point. Because it is no longer I who speak.

J.N.: Just the same, there is something strange in your entire story. Why, when you were in Bangladesh and looking for spiritual advice or discernment following the messages you were receiving, did you look for it in a Catholic seminary? Wasn't there a Greek Orthodox Church?

V.: There was none at all. The Lord made it easy for me; the city of Dhaka is quite large and traffic is chaotic, yet the house where I lived was next to the Catholic Church. There was an Armenian Orthodox Church in the city but very far. In five minutes I was with the Catholics.

J.N.: So it's simply a matter of circumstances, we might say providential, that you in a certain way went to them?

V.: I'm pleased that you use the word "providential." You didn't say, "You were lucky." Because, once, the Lord told me, "There is no such word as 'luck' in my vocabulary."

J.N.: So, there is no "by chance." Chance does not exist. But everything can be taken as chance because, otherwise, it becomes oppressive. Man would have no more freedom. Let's get on to another subject. Is there, in the messages you receive, a statement concerning the Jews?

V.: Yes. I had a message because I asked once: "What about the Jews and the Muslims? What do you think of them?" And the Lord told me: "Pray for them because I love them as much as I love you."

J.N.: What do you think of the rampant anti-Semitism in Europe? What do you think of this feeling of hatred toward the Jews that developed in Christian countries, in France or in Germany, for centuries, which started the massacre of the Second World War and is making a comeback?

V.: Hatred does not come from God. It comes from Satan; from Satan, yes.

J.N.: The same for the Muslims?

V.: Absolutely. The persecutions against the Jews and the Muslims in the past, and now, have a satanic origin. God has never divided us. All those who practice a religion are equally dear to God. It's not enough to belong to the Roman Catholic or Orthodox Church to be saved. Those who do not belong to these churches are no less God's creatures made in His Image. Salvation is promised to all those who obey God's Commandments. Jesus was crucified for all mankind. To the one who has received much, God will ask more. That is what is special about being Christian. It's not a privilege but an extra obligation on their part. When all is said, God is the only judge; He is love and He will judge according to the love men have shown on earth.

J.N.: I would also like to ask you a question about the unbelievers. Basically, the messages you get are for those who come to hear you. I would not say you are preaching to the converted, there are conversions, but still they are people who have a Christian background, an embryo of education and sensitivity. And then there are the unbelievers of our modern society who have never received any religious education. Do you receive messages especially for unbelievers, atheists?

V.: I do not receive specific calls for such and such a category. It is a universal call that is destined even to the converted so that they convert completely. In the meetings I have been holding during these past years, there are atheists who are interested because they have read the messages and want to know more about them from me. But there are also persons who were absolute atheists, or rather apostates, who the Lord has brought back. We have all the prayer groups that have been formed in Greece; each one could give a testimony. All had left the church. They were apostates. Others nourish hatred against priests. When they saw a priest they would cross over to the other side of the street not to find themselves on the same side. All those were brought back to the faith through what the Lord says in the messages. These messages touch the heart, awakens those who were dead, and then bring them back home.

J.N.: Could we say that it is bad Christians that are brought back to God?

V.: They are not bad. They are the victims of society. It's not their fault. A bad Christian is one whose heart is hard as stone and cannot be broken. Whereas the victims of society are floating; they don't know where to go. When you tell them, "There, the Lord is at your door."—"But I have never prayed, why does He come? Is He looking at me, too? I thought He only went to those who love Him." At last they find in the message something that awakens them.

J.N.: Let's come around to the prophecy about John Paul II's successor that you mention sometimes. Have you an idea about what is going to happen?

V.: No. The Lord never says anything to me. I know there is a problem within the church; apostasy, and rebellion against this pope. The Lord says that the rebellion has penetrated into the sanctuary itself. Cardinal Ratzinger has even repeated something Pope Paul VI said about Satan's smoke having penetrated the sanctuary. This spirit of rebellion denies Christ. And it is not only denying Christ as such, it is denying the divinity of Christ.

J.N.: There are, in particular, theologians who deny the divinity of Jesus.

V.: They are the Antichrists of today.

J.N.: The message tells you that they have penetrated as far as the heart of the Catholic Church or is it simply theologians who profess this heresy?

V.: No, in the heart; in the sanctuary.

J.N.: In the sanctuary? Could you be more specific?

V.: No, because if I could, I would have given specifics, but I do not have specifics. As for me, I think that the sanctuary is really the church.

J.N.: It could be only at the level of schools of theology, seminaries?

V.: Undoubtedly, it could be. But it's more serious than that. According to Paul VI, it is the sanctuary itself.

J.N.: You know that there is a dogma of papal infallibility that says that in certain well-defined circumstances, the pope cannot err. Do you sometimes receive messages related to papal infallibility?

V.: The word has really never been used, but the Lord speaks about the respect due to the Vicar of the Church, to the one who represents Christ on earth. All that concerns the pope must be respected, including the dogma of infallibility.

J.N.: You know that within the church there are all kinds of controversies over the ordination of women and their possible right to celebrate the Eucharist?

V.: The Lord has not given me any message on that subject.

J.N.: He has not spoken on that subject? So, neither for nor against?

V.: Neither for nor against. When the Lord chooses someone for a mission, He does not burden him with all the problems of the church; He gives him a particular message. For other problems He chooses someone else. My mission is uniquely a call to conversion, to unity and to reconciliation. The pope is opposed to the ordination of women and, as I mentioned before, we must obey him.

J.N.: Let's get back to the problem of unity.

V.: Our division is a sin. Division does not come from God but from the *"diabolos,"* a Greek word meaning the one who brings division, translated into English as "devil." First of all, the greatest desire of Christ regarding unity—and which will also be the key to unity—is the unification of the date of Easter, done in humility and with love. On October 26, 1989, Christ called me and asked me to draw three iron bars, each one with a head on top. So I drew three bars, adding a head as He had indicated. He told me that these three iron bars represented the Roman Catholics, the Orthodox, and the Protestants. Then He told me that He wanted these churches to bend and unite. But He added:

These iron bars are still very stiff and cannot bend on their own, so I shall have to come to them with My Fire and with the power of My

Flame upon them they shall turn soft to bend and mould into one solid iron bar, and My Glory will fill the whole earth.

But unity is not merchandise and to reach unity we must not become merchants. Christ will expel the merchants from His Church as He did in the temple of Jerusalem. Neither does Christ like the vague chumminess that is often going on before His Eyes, in the name of unity. That's a false ecumenism. Christ often complains about the lack of sincerity among those who are working for unity.

False ecumenism amounts to selling out certain truths to create a superficial unity. Many people accuse me of inducing a drawing together of Orthodox and Catholic denominations and leaving aside the Protestants. Well, I've met many pastors, in Sweden for example, who are very attracted to the messages in favor of unity. They realize that they have made certain errors in neglecting the Blessed Virgin. True ecumenism requires that we point out to them that Luther brought deeper insights on certain points, such as the use of Scripture, but that he also neglected certain truths. It would be necessary to go back and recover the Tradition that existed before the Reformation. The message is not easy to communicate but we must go through that. False ecumenism consists in pretending to agree, to be pals on the surface. It's unfortunately quite common in Switzerland where certain Catholic priests and Protestant pastors meet and fail to invite the Orthodox. As if they were afraid the Orthodox would remind them of certain embarrassing truths which they share with the Catholics but not with the Protestants, truths which are silenced in the official ecumenical dialog. That explains why, in a certain way, my presence is disturbing.

Unity will be achieved through the conversion of the heart, through a call from the Holy Spirit so that He may be our only guide and the lamp in our soul. Unity will come about through humility and love. Unity will be achieved when we really begin to love Christ. Unity will be achieved when everyone dies to himself. Unity will be achieved when we begin to lower our voices in order to hear Christ's voice; when we begin to lower our heads in order to see Christ's head, and only when we bow down completely will we see God's will. Unity will be achieved when we look after the interests of Christ and the Church and not our own. Unity will be achieved by keeping the Tradition as it was taught us by the Fathers of the Church and not by trading or selling it. To achieve unity, we have to safeguard the faith and follow, to the letter, the holy sacraments of the church; this is how we will be able to restore unity according to Christ's wishes, and the words of His priestly prayer will be accomplished, "That all may be one as the Father and I are one."

That is why, when I give testimony before crowds, I first call for the conversion of our heart, because we cannot unite if we do not love. With love we can arrive at reconciliation and forgiveness. We can base everything on love. Love is the foundation upon which reconciliation and unity are built. In one of His messages, God gave me to understand that a good tree is rooted in love. On every branch of this tree there will be fruits, and He compared the fruits to virtues. So long as we will not forgive, God's blessings cannot reach us.

Since the subject of unity is a very important one, allow me to give you a few quotations from His Messages.

In an interior vision, I saw the Blessed Virgin sitting on a small white rock. She was bent over, her face hidden on her knees. She was dressed in black like the Lady of Sorrows. I saw her from the back and approached her from her left. As I was coming near she looked up and saw me. I saw her face, pale but very beautiful, torn with sorrow; it was filled with tears. Her eyes were of a transparent, clear blue color. And she told me:

Treason barricades unity among brothers, insincerity of heart induces God's Cup to augment; they wrenched the Body of My Son, divided It, mutilated It and paralyzed It;

I am reminding you all that through Him, all of you have in the One Spirit your way to come to the Father, yet you remain divided under My Son's Name; you speak of unity and peace and yet stretch a net for those who practice it; God cannot be deceived nor is He convinced by your arguments;

The Kingdom of God is not just words on the lips, the Kingdom of God is love, peace, unity, and faith in the heart: it is the Lord's Church united in One inside your heart;

The Keys to Unity are: Love and Humility; Jesus never urged you to divide yourselves, this division in His Church was no desire of His. I implore My children to unite in heart and voice and rebuild My Son's primitive Church in their heart; I am saying My Son's primitive Church, since that Church was constructed on Love, Simplicity, Humility and Faith;

I do not mean you to reconstruct a new edifice, I mean you to reconstruct an edifice inside your heart, I mean you to knock down the old bricks inside your heart, bricks of disunion, intolerance, unfaithfulness, unforgiveness, lack of love, and reconstruct My Son's Church by reconciling; you need intense poverty of the spirit and an overflow of wealth of generosity, and not until you understand that you will have to bend, will you be able to unite. (September 23, 1991)

Christ suffers mystically from our division and He becomes very stern when He sees lack of sincerity. He does not mince words when He speaks to those who prefer to remain divided. He is stern with those who pretend to work for unity, but who, in fact, work for their own interests only. Here is what He says:

And now I make a special appeal to all those who are under My Name and are working for Unity and Peace; I ask you to come to Me like a child and face Me answering Me these questions: "brothers, have you done everything you can to preserve the unity of My Body?" (March 10, 1990)

Every Easter season I must drink from the cup of your division since this cup is forced on Me; but you too, daughter, will drink from it; you shall share with Me what is bitter—given by human hand; the more time passes for them to unite the dates of Easter, the more severe will be the sentence this generation will receive; My Return is imminent and woe to the unrepentant heart! woe to the divided heart! woe to the unreconciled heart! "they shall be thrown down to hell!" Mat. 11:23 (May 31, 1994)

By staying divided we are exactly like the dry bones of the prophet Ezekiel's oracle. If we do not allow the Holy Spirit to blow on us, we will remain like dry bones, strewn in the valley of the dead. But if we allow the Holy Spirit to blow on us, we will come to life as well. The Holy Spirit will put sinews on us and grow flesh on our bones. He will stretch skin over us and we shall become a whole body... Then the Holy Spirit will blow again on us to revive us and we shall stand upright. And this way God shall be glorified.

On August 11, 1996, during the Angelus, Pope John Paul II, speaking of the Orthodox, said: "The things that unite us are stronger than that which divide us." John Paul II speaks and writes a lot about the Orthodox. His voice reminds me of John the Baptist, a voice crying out in the desert—the desert of our heart—for unity with the Orthodox. But then, why do we not hear in our churches from priests, bishops, and cardinals the slightest echo of that voice? Why isn't anything being done to make it resound and awaken the dead? Why aren't they joining their voices to that of the pope? In all honesty, I think that the pope doesn't get enough support regarding unity with the Orthodox.

One day Christ came and confided to me, "I burn with a desire." I asked Him then what His desire was and He told me: "To see My Church united and one." He added:

It is not the eloquence of speech nor the lengthy discourse that will lead them to unity; it is not their exchange of praise on one another that will lead My Church into one; all these things weary Me...devastation and ruin have penetrated into My Sanctuary, so what praise can they exchange on one another? Where is their honor? Bow down that you may see My Will; lower your voice so that you hear Salvation speaking to you from the heights of glory; It is in your conversion that your heart will hear Me and lead My Church into one, unifying My Body; it is in the splendor of the Truth that you will fragrance again and make everyone recognize themself as part of one body.

Ah...daughter, pray for the house of the East and the West to join together, like two hands when joined in prayer, a pair of hands, similar, and in beauty when joined together pointing toward heaven when in prayer; let those two Hands, belonging to the same body work together and share their capacity and resources with each other...let those two Hands lift Me together, ah...when will those Hands of My Body lift Me over the Altar, holding Me together? O come! (June 15, 1995)

Throughout His messages on unity, Christ begs, calls, cries out, implores, weeps for His Church to unite, and if He repeats Himself so often it is because of our deafness. "I want incense from their heart, I want peace from their heart, I want praises from their heart—I want love, mercy, and compassion from their heart. I want reconciliation from their heart..." That is how He is calling to us.

Chapter Fourteen

Holy Russia

V.: I heard the word Russia for the first time, in the messages, two years before the fall of Communism.

J.N.: What was that message?

V.: It seemed as if God's voice was sending an urgent call to show us that God had a very great sorrow. And He calls me, "Vassula, come and look!" Then He takes me in spirit to see the vision, "Come and look! Your sister is dead." When He said: "Your sister," I knew very well that He was not talking about my own sisters. "Your sister Russia is dead." I could see myself in a flat desert. There was a woman lying on the ground. She was dead and holding something in her hand, a fruit. I didn't even see what kind of fruit it was. God said to me, "Your sister is dead." And I understood at that moment that he was calling Russia my sister because she is Orthodox.

J.N.: It's obvious.

V.: From the beginning, when God spoke about Russia He never spoke of her as a country but as His daughter, Russia; His beloved daughter, Russia. And He told me: "She is dead." And when I saw her I burst into tears. I couldn't stop the tears because I felt two things at the same time. First, I felt that she was really my sister and that I loved her. And then the sorrow of her father, God. It was immeasurable. And it made me cry very much. So He told me, "O do not weep; I will resurrect her Vassula; I will resur-

rect her for My Glory; I will revive her as I have revived Lazarus."
Then He began to tell me of her fall, always in symbolic terms.
His daughter who was faithful started putting on airs and then she
sold her gifts, that is, the churches. Finally she turned to the enemy who betrayed her. But God told it in a very beautiful way. I
listened to this story as if it was about one of His faithful daughters who had finally decided to take a wrong path. She went away
and since that time has known only misfortune. God told me,
"Anyway, I have plans for her because Russia shall glorify Me more
than any other nation. She will become the spiritual head of all
other countries, all other nations. She will glorify Me." Afterwards,
He was speaking about her as if He was going to bring her back
holding her by the arm like a father who is proud of His daughter
and wants to show her off to everybody.

*J.N.: You were told this story two years before the fall of the
Berlin Wall. At the time Communism collapsed, what were the
messages?*

V.: At that time He told me: "I will resurrect her as I did with
Lazarus. Now I am near her, warming up her heart which is very
cold." I had a vision in which He had His hand upon this woman
to warm up her heart. And He told me: "I will transfigure her as I
was transfigured." I can't describe exactly the rest of the prophecy. It's better not to talk too much about it as it is a very dangerous subject. I will quote texts later on. Many prophecies about
Russia have already been fulfilled. God has given her freedom,
but Russia still has a choice. If she perverts this freedom, God
will send Russia a very severe tribulation. I'm wondering if it wasn't
the war in Chechnya.

J.N.: Really? The Chechen war?

V.: It's possible, because this warning came before the war.

Spiritually Russia is making progress, but there is a lot of corruption. Maybe God wished to purify her even more.

J.N.: I remember that the Berlin Wall fell on November 9, 1989. Do you have prior texts?

V.:   Yes. I have kept all the texts about Russia.

Russia is a nation very dear to the Lord. On July 13, 1917, in Fatima the Virgin Mary said:

If you do as I say, many souls will be saved and you will have peace! War will end. But if you do not stop offending God, under the reign of Pius XI another one will begin, even worse. When you see an unknown light on a bright night, know that it is the great sign God is giving you, that He is going to punish the world for its crimes through war, famine and persecutions against the Church and the Holy Father. In order to avoid this I will come to ask for the Consecration of Russia to My Immaculate Heart and Communion on the first Saturdays in reparation. If you heed My requests, Russia will convert and there will be peace. If not, she will propagate her errors throughout the world, bringing wars and persecutions against the Church. The good will be martyred, the Holy Father will suffer greatly, and many nations will be annihilated. In the end my Immaculate Heart will triumph. The Holy Father will consecrate Russia to me and she will convert, and a certain time of peace will be given to the world. In Portugal the dogma of the faith will always be preserved. And I shall return here, in the same way, for a seventh time.

But after the sufferings and purification Russia has known, the Lord is now proclaiming that she is the nation through which God will be the most glorified.

In *True Life in God,* I have received many prophecies about Russia and some of them have already been fulfilled.

On October 31, 1989, as I was praying at home, in front of Our Lady of Fatima statue, I leaned toward the statue and I whispered these words inspired by the Holy Spirit:

You know, Jesus gave me something very precious to guard. It has to do with the glorification of His Body. It also is for the salvation of souls! So I come to you, dear mother, to ask you if you could keep It, guard It and defend It for me. Yes, it is the Lord's Revelation; I entirely handed It over into your hands. In the meantime, I must carry on the work of the Sacred Heart of Jesus, He Who has raised me up for this mission and Who has formed me.

In my notebook I added this commentary:

Soon, at the sound of His voice, the dead will raise from their graves, all for His Glory. Soon a nation will resurrect, a nation consecrated to His Holy Name, for this has been made known a long time ago.

Of course the nation I was talking about was Russia.

But already on January 4, 1988, I had received the following call from God where sadness mingled with urgency.

"O Vassula! I have one of My beloved daughters lying dead! A sister of yours!"

"Who's lying dead, Lord?"

"My well-beloved daughter Russia. Come! Come and I will show her to you. Look!"

And then I saw the vision I described at the beginning. I told Him I was very sad. But right away He told me,

O do not weep, I will resurrect her Vassula, I will resurrect her for My Glory, I will revive her as I have revived Lazarus.

This pain you feel is nothing compared to Mine. I love her Vassula, have pity on her too, I will not leave her lying dead and exposed in the scorching winds. Vassula, love your sister; pity her, go to her, love her, love her, for she is so unloved by everyone!

Vassula, she had abandoned Me and turned against Me; She turned against Me when she grew, and when it was her time for love I called her to share My cloak but instead she walked away, feeling mature, she believed she would be able to feed herself on her own, she turned her back to Me and walked away, like an unfaithful wife she fled. My beloved do you know what it is like losing a daughter? My Heart lacerated, I wept.

Like this was not enough, she proudly and without the slightest remorse declared openly war against Me her Father and against all the martyr Saints! She believed in Me no more; she stopped worshipping Me, hoping in Me, and loving Me! She seemed to have forgotten the love we once shared; I had given her sons and daughters but in her fury she slaughtered My children and handed them over to Satan as one offers a burnt offering.

Then, as though this was not enough, she turned to Satan and made a pact with him to be faithful to him and worship him instead, if he would offer her all what she desired. Satan agreed with the condition to leave him free. Satan then disconnected her entirely from Me; she let him cut our bonds, he made her trust him; treacherous as he is, he led My daughter into marshlands first, where she would <u>have</u> to lean on him; from fear of sinking into quicksand; she asked him to allow her to lean <u>entirely</u> on him,

Vassula, like Jerusalem at one time who fled from My House, My House of Holiness to become a daughter of no morals, offering her children one after the other as a sacrifice, Russia, My daughter, thought it wise to do the same, she took My Holy Presents, offering them to Satan who turned them all into weapons. Satan blinded her with his glory and in her blindness removed her from the marshlands and placed her into the wilderness to thirst and die.

I saw her walking naked and struggling in her own blood, I called her, but she would not listen (at Fatima?), I called her again, but she would not hear My call, instead, she provoked Me, calling her younger sisters to support her morals, if they refused she forced them with her sword, have I not said, "He who will raise the sword shall perish by the sword"?

I rationed her bread so that she would need My Bread, but she preferred to starve rather than eat from Me. Exhausted and hungered, she sent her younger sisters to continue her wicked works in secret, because her vanity was inspired by <u>Vanity himself who is Satan</u>. Her lands bore not enough to feed her; she became as one would say, "a dependent" on My enemy." (January 4, 1988)

The following day when I read again the passage about Russia lying dead, I cried bitter tears again. Then Jesus told me:

When Russia became a dependent of Satan because her land was barren, he offered her the deadly fruit he keeps in store for those I love. It kills in stages; the more one eats of it the more one needs it. It's deadly; killing slowly. He nourished her with his fruit and killed her; she died with this fruit still clenched in her hand.

Vassula trust Me, I will resurrect her. Daughter be still, do not worry, leave Me free and I will accomplish My Works. (January 5, 1988)

On November 13 and 14, 1989, I received another prophecy on Russia that has since been realized:

O Russia! mere creature of flesh! evil coiled in your very womb, creature of mere dust and ashes, I the Most High shall resurrect you for I am the Resurrection, I shall nurse you back to Life and I shall with My Finger upon you, transfigure you into a glorious nation as I was transfigured, you shall be majestically dressed in dazzling white robes and all Heaven shall thrust away Its mourning garments and Heaven's bitter Tears shall turn into joyful tears, all Heaven will celebrate your Resurrection and all the martyr-saints who prayed without cease by the Feet of your Holy Mother for Her intercession, shall in this day too, together with My Mother and Her innumerable holy angels, all descend in your children's homes and make their home together with them. I then shall feed them My Body and offer them My Blood to drink; Russia shall eat Me and drink Me with great love, praising Me; My Russia shall be the living example of your times and for generations to come, because of her Great Conversion. (November 13/14, 1989)

It's not by chance that the Lord said in His message: "I shall transfigure you into a glorious nation as I was transfigured." In fact, the putsch that sealed the fall of communism in Russia took place on Sunday, August 19, 1991, the day the Russian Orthodox Church celebrates the feast of Transfiguration. Later in the same prophecy, the Lord said:

Hence a covenant of Peace and Love shall be signed and sealed between Me and her. I love her and always have, even in her disloyalty toward Me and even in her wickedness I blessed her and blessed her. This shall be My Glorious Miracle; just wait and see; those who have fallen asleep in hatred, hating Me for no reason, those too I shall bring back to life since they are her sons too and still live in her womb; all these things shall soon take place. (November 13/14, 1989)

This means that never again will Russia deny our God.

Three years later, on September 9, 1992, I received from the Lord another encouraging prophecy regarding Russia:

Those who are far away will come and repent; they will rebuild My Church and I for My part will anoint each heart, and as someone roused from his sleep, Russia, will rouse quivering with impatience to be consumed by Me; I will deliver you and place you as head of many nations; foreigners will grow faint of heart upon seeing your beauty. (September 9, 1992)

The following month, on October 20, 1992, the Lord said:

Russia, it is not long ago since you broke your alliance with Me, burst your bonds and said: "I will not serve You!" Now I shall give you children who will proclaim My Name in Holiness and say: "Blessed is He who restored our sight and touched our heart; blessed is He who changed our ways healing us;" then, with Me in you and you in Me, you will live and with Our Two Hearts in your heart you will give Me the Glory foretold.

In the same prophecy the Lord says:

"Soon the Glory will be given to Me in its fullness and Russia will govern the rest of My children in holiness."

What does our Lord want to tell us by that? Is He telling us that after the unification of the churches is accomplished, a pope from the Eastern Church will emerge? It is always difficult to interpret prophecies, even for me who receives prophesies, I would never dare try to decipher them without the Lord clarifying it for me. But the future will tell by itself the prophecies regarding Russia which have not yet been fulfilled.

Nevertheless, the prophecies about Russia are impressive in their triumphant tone, especially this one,

My beloved [Russia], there your shepherds' noble voices will call out:

"Salvation! Priests and ministers of the Most High, salvation will only be found in Love! Peace! shepherds of the Reflection of the Father, peace will only be found in Forgiveness; Unity! unity, brothers of the Light thrice holy and Who is One in Three, Three in One Light, will only be found by intermarrying! May our Lord Almighty, the Irresistible One, render us worthy of His Name, may He grant us to be one in His Name; Eternal Father, let us be so completely one that the rest of the world will realize that it was You who sent the Sacrificial Lamb to glorify You and have Your Name known." (December 13, 1993)

One might say that it is through Russia that unity will come. However this prophecy is accompanied with conditions:

Russia, your role is to honor Me and glorify Me; the Festivity has yet to come, but it depends from you in which manner that Day will come: do not let Me make you return to Me by fire, but with bonds of Peace. (December 13, 1993)

CHAPTER FIFTEEN

Everyday Life

J.N.: Would you talk about money? Not just money but all the goods that we are trying to acquire and pile up today, the latest television set, video recorder, computer, skiing or diving equipment, etc.

V.:   We must not identify ourselves with what we possess, yet it is necessary to manage goods; after all I am a mother and housewife. However, we have to learn not to become attached to material goods and not pile them up.

J.N.: Should we impose on ourselves the rule of poverty? I know a Benedictine monastery where monks earn money selling the various things they produce from their work, which allows them to provide for their daily needs. But they always keep a little reserve ahead. The rule, I have been told, consists in having enough to provide for one year and giving away all the rest.

V.:   I didn't know such a rule existed.

J.N.: Do you have an opinion on that subject? Should we apply such a rule in the home? That is to say, never stocking up beyond that?

V.:   As for monks, I think they should be able to trust a little bit more in God, for the day to day. Jesus told us in the Scriptures the parable of the birds in the air and the flax in the fields that neither spin nor weave and are more sumptuously attired than King Solomon. But in the world we live in today we cannot say

"Insh' Allah" [God willing] <u>all</u> the time. We mustn't exaggerate either way. We must reach a balance. And that balance always pleases God. In Scriptures He says, "Do always that which is right!" All that is right—no more and no less. From that standpoint a year's provision; that may be right. But I was surprised when you told me that.

J.N.: Why are you surprised?

V.: I am surprised because I thought monks would rely more on God. When Jesus sent out His apostles on a mission, He told them: "Take nothing for the journey, no staff, no bag, no bread, no money, no extra tunic." I know a story about a charismatic group formerly known as The Lion of Judah, now The Beatitudes. They had no more money. Not even for a month. They sat down to eat but had no food. And then someone knocks at the door just as they were praying, "You told us to trust, we want to thank you even in front of an empty plate." The person at the door brought them lots of food. They received at that very moment the food they needed. But they did not stock up, not even for one week.

J.N.: So, in your opinion, a monastery that would have this small reserve exaggerates in terms of prudence and precaution?

V.: I do not know. I think I could live from day to day in a monastery, if I were in a monastery. I have known missionaries who are in Africa, in India, in Bangladesh who have nothing. They are like beggars. And you? Your opinion?

J.N.: If I were a religious I would leave that concern to the Superior or the steward.

V.: And if you were the Superior or the steward? Would you put aside a reserve to live on for a year?

J.N.: If I were the Superior this is the kind of rule I would adopt.

V.: To be sure of the future?

J.N.: To be sure of the future. To be prepared for anything that could happen. But it's probably because I do not have enough faith. One of the saints I most admire is St. Francis. No other saint came as close to Jesus as St. Francis. I admire him because I would never manage to live as he lived. How can we achieve this ideal today when manipulation through advertising leads families to spend a lot of money for things that are far from essential? There are necessities for everyday life, food, clothes, and heating. But what should be our attitude toward the superfluous? I'm thinking of a very powerful car, I'm thinking of expensive furniture, antique paintings, silver, gourmet food, and costly wines. Does this coincide really with a life of prayer or is it an obstacle?

V.:   I have experienced very well-to-do people who have found no hindrance in their wealth to lead a life of spirituality. They have a fine house, but their spiritual life is very deep. They acknowledge that all they have comes from God. There is no contradiction. They are very charitable toward the churches, toward charitable works; they are really very generous. Their possessions are blessings from God who has given them health and money in the same way. They are practicing charity according to the Gospel that says that faith without good works is sterile and that there is greater joy in giving than in receiving. I also know well-to-do people who count every penny and are not charitable. They are wicked and selfish. They do not have a spiritual life. They have rejected God, irrespective of their fortune.

J.N.: Now, I would now like to talk a little bit about work. You do not talk about work as such in True Life in God. *Now, we all work; most adults work the greater part of the day, one way or another, within or outside the home. So I don't have anything to ask you about work itself, but I would like to hear what you have to say about work, about the disproportionate focus so-*

ciety puts on paid employment. To survive in our society obsessed with productivity, a father must work hard and work well, otherwise he may lose his job. Once he has lost his job and is out of a normal career, it will be hard for him to get back into the production machinery. There is good reason to suffer anxiety. What do you think of the situation we are in nowadays?

V.: I think that society asks too much, more and more; every year it gets worse. It's like a knot tightening more and more. The person who is not at the same income level as his neighbor feels inferior. So everyone is working himself to death. And finally human nature can no longer resist, because it is not normal, and it goes beyond our nature. Stress, suicide, depression, addiction to alcohol, tobacco, narcotics, drugs. It's not normal. I think it's too much. We need a change that consists in rediscovering God. I hope heaven will help us. Because it's out of the question that the young study a number of years to learn a profession or trade and then cannot find work.

J.N.: So frenetic work is not a value, it's the opposite?

V.: It is the sins of the world that have brought about this situation in which we are caught up.

J.N.: For example, competition such as we see it, within an enterprise where everyone tries to climb over the heads of others, do you think it's wrong?

V.: It's selfishness, radically contrary to the Second Commandment that enjoins us to love our neighbor. We do the opposite. If the world followed God's commandments, this would not have happened. The present crisis is proof that the world is living without God.

J.N.: Let's be quite down-to-earth, let's take the case of a firm where two people are competing for the same post and the one who loses the promotion also loses his place in society and tenure at an age when he cannot find another one. Could a staunch Christian use all possible means, including the most dishonest ones, in order to preserve the money he must earn for his family, and spare them poverty in our unmerciful society? Should he engage in that competition or must he accept in advance that he will lose out to a dishonest rival; lose his job and become unemployed? This is asking him to be heroic.

V.: Someone who is converted and lives in God cannot become dishonest. He cannot. He cannot believe that his duty is to be dishonest. He is willing to suffer, placing his trust in God who will not desert him.

J.N.: Is there a way to work hard?

V.: When we love God, everything becomes easy. Even the hardest tasks. And we always perform them with joy. Even a difficult and boring task, because we feel such a joy that no one can take from us. It's God's joy and hope in us. In spite of all the difficult problems around us, we face these problems perhaps with more courage.

J.N.: Should we work harder and do better than most because this work is being offered to God?

V.: It depends on the person. Some are perfectionists. It is not because one is converted that one becomes perfect. Conversion is like a stairway going up toward heaven. Every step brings us closer to heaven in augmenting the climber's perfection.

J.N.: Let's examine another facet of everyday life. Now, I would like you to talk about something that is a problem for many people now. Many couples are breaking up. Do the messages speak sometimes about the difficulties of living together?

V.: The messages sometimes speak of the harmony of couples

and their unity. There are many divorces now because God is not part of the family. If the two people who join in marriage were bound to God and in God, they would not separate, because division does not come from God. In Greek, the word *"diabolos"*—devil, means he who divides. A family centered on God constitutes the ideal environment for educating children in religion. It would be an ideal family. Unfortunately, things do not happen that way. In my own family, before my conversion, things weren't going as they should. Today, I can see that it was the absence of God that divided my family.

J.N.: That is true not only for married couples, but also for children. In your opinion, is it possible to properly care for children within the family, to give them a proper education outside of all religious reference?

V.: In her messages, the Blessed Virgin Mary says that we must bring up our children from the very first with religion. However, without violating their freedom as this could have the opposite effect. Faith must be taught according to the soul's capacity. It's like glasses, some are small, some are large. We must fill the glass, but not to overflowing. A small glass does not have the same capacity as a large glass. This is how we must treat children in their spiritual education. When this education is started much later, when they are fifteen or sixteen and have never received any spiritual training, it is very difficult to bring them into religion. They might do it in spite of themselves, because their parents demand it; they will do it, but grudgingly. Now my sons, when I converted, one was ten, and the other fifteen. The fifteen-year-old didn't quite agree. But the ten-year-old, I could still educate him in the faith.

J.N.: There are some theories in education that recommend the absence of all religious education for children so as to leave them free to choose when they are adults.

V.: It never works. They even go further and suggest not to baptize children so that they may be free to choose when they grow up. I do not agree because they will refuse later. Why? Because they have no idea concerning faith, they do not know. When they are educated from a tender age, they can always choose from full knowledge and refuse freely a faith they know. Such is true freedom of choice. Besides, if they have been educated in the faith a seed has already been planted and they will have a certain experience of spirituality even if it does not run deep. It can only do them good.

I also insist on prayer for the young. If the parents are churchgoers, and not just out of duty or because of social pressure, if they really think they are living in God, well these families normally pray the rosary together with the children. I know many. They are families that really live in love and unity with their children. If the children are bored by a rosary, because they do not yet understand that it is an exercise in meditation, if they find it repetitive and boring, you should suggest only one mystery. I have asked the Blessed Virgin to intervene. I admitted it was my fault if my children had not been educated in the faith, but that I needed her help. I consecrated my children to the Blessed Virgin Mary and she did everything. She has done miracles with my sons to have them return to a life of prayer. For example, my younger son asked me once why God has given so much power to Satan. I replied that Satan is very powerful but that we can fight him with prayer. When we pray he runs away. The rosary can put him in chains because it is a chain. For my son, as with all children, fascinating stories are stories where the good must win and the bad must lose. There's always a way to convince the young.

J.N.: Should we, and at what age, start introducing children and then teenagers to the reading of the Bible?

V.: If there are schools that provide religious education, we should start when they are eight or nine years old.

J.N.: Should we, and at what age, start taking children to religious ceremonies which are mostly practiced for adults?

V.: What ceremonies? Mass?

J.N.: Mass, for example. Does it have any meaning and at what age should we take them? Should we force them?

V.: In an Orthodox Church there is no minimum age. There are babies, there are two-year-olds, and they keep quiet. Maybe they do not listen, because they are children, but they get accustomed. They begin to get accustomed. And I think the earlier the better.

J.N.: If a youth turns out to be quite rebellious, let's say from adolescence, around fifteen, is there a time when he should be left alone?

V.: We should use reason. If he rebels against his school we aren't going to take him out of school and leave him without education. His parents try to reason with him to go to school. And we should also pray, because there is power in prayer. If we pray for someone who rebels, God answers us in the end.

J.N.: More generally, considering young adults, those who are still studying, those who are just out of school, we notice a kind of generalized apostasy. There is not one in ten or one in twenty who attends church on a regular basis. Would you have some advice for those who try nevertheless to get them interested? As a rule, we are up against their indifference. They are totally indifferent and totally ignorant. How can we catch their interest?

V.: I think they are more ignorant than negative. Ignorance has a negative side because they are under the impression that religion is for the old. And this is quite untrue. They think religion is boring. And it's not that at all, because once they meet God, I can attest, they discover joy. So they should try to meet God, because then they will meet the One who loves them the most and they will discover a life totally changed.

J.N.: I would like to discuss a final aspect of everyday life, which we cannot avoid. Politics. Citizens must care about the city they live in, and even about what is going on elsewhere. Do you think that politics today are what they should be?

V.:   In your opinion, are they? I do not think they are, because of all the wars. There is shooting everywhere. And the Lord talks about that in His messages. This is not what He Himself wants. And so, He is against all these conflicts. It all comes down to the same thing. Love is missing, since it is love that brings peace, unity, and harmony. It is said that at the end of times, the world will become ice-cold when it comes to the love of God and that heaven will have to intervene. This is what God is doing today.

J.N.: Many commentators observe that, in all those wars, religion plays an important role. This is the case in Northern Ireland where Catholics and Protestants fight each other. It's the case in Lebanon where Muslims and Christians are murdered. It was the case in Yugoslavia, where Catholics, Orthodox, and Muslims exterminated each other. It's the case in Algeria where Christians are murdered by Muslims. Some people who do not like religion very much say that it is a cause of conflict rather than a source of peace.

V.:   This is an excuse. Religion goes much deeper than that. They bring up religion as an excuse.

J.N.: What is the real cause?

V.:   There are many causes. As I am not a politician, I cannot talk about it.

J.N.: What is the spiritual cause of wars? Is war a spiritual disease? Is it a lack of faith in God? Or a certain faith in a certain God?

V.: That's not the cause.

J.N.: But this perverted faith seems to be the cause.

V.: At first sight. But religion is not the cause.

J.N.: What about the genocide of Jews by Christians during the war?

V.: Hitler wasn't exactly a model Christian. There are lots of examples of conflicts. In Egypt, Christians are persecuted by Muslim extremists.

J.N.: Precisely. That suggests that religion leads to violence.

V.: I've seen it. In Egypt, when churches begin to fall into ruin, when they have deteriorated and need repairs, the law forbids to even paint them over. Why? Because they want them to crumble completely and be done with the Christians. They build a mosque. You can't visit a church without seeing a mosque facing it.

J.N.: We can also see the same thing in Palestine. The Christian community in Palestine that was quite small, a few thousands, is disappearing because of the Israeli government's hostility toward the Palestinians, Christians, and Muslims alike. Finally, you are well aware that during this century, more specifically since the end of the Second World War, most wars have had religious ramifications, or religious excuses, or religious pretexts. Populations speaking the same language and from the same ethnic background are fighting each other merely on the basis of their religious affiliation.

V.: It's always a pretext. I am sure of it. You only have to listen to the testimonies of lay people from different religions who were living in peace. In ex-Yugoslavia, religion was used as an alibi for those who wanted war anyhow.

J.N.: But you have no explanation? Among the spiritual evils of our time, you cannot acknowledge that these wars may have a religious origin?

V.: No, I do not have any comment on the subject. Christ has not come to teach us the art of good politics. It's useless to try to find answers to your questions in the messages I have received. Every time I've touched on this question, the Lord has kept silent, as if to remind us that the essential thing is to convert and from that conversion, peace will follow.

J.N.: So everyday life is not easy for Christians. How do you feel about being still on this earth?

V.: Now my life is not easy; it is definitely split in two since my conversion. Here on earth, I feel like an exile and I long for heaven, to meet my Father, the Son, and the Holy Spirit. All I do now is for the glory of God and my life is centered on God alone. If the Lord had not allowed me to touch His Heart and see His Riches, if He had not granted me countless favors, I would have had neither the courage nor the strength to continue, serenely and in peace, the work He has assigned to me on this earth. Also, I would not have been able to endure the trials, the criticism, the opposition, the false witnesses, and the assaults from the devil if God had not showered me with extraordinary favors in order to help me with my mission and so help me overcome all those trials. But the Lord stands by my side and always reminds me of those words He spoke to me once, words that He spoke for all of us, and I would like to quote here:

Vassula, happy are those who withdraw from their occupations and follow Me. You are indeed devoting a lot of your time writing with Me, but let Me tell you something else too. I also love to see you work and accomplish minor duties, duties of small importance, as long as you do them with love. Every little work you do, no matter how small and meaningless becomes great in My Eyes and pleases Me, as long as these small acts are done with love. Be blessed. (February 18, 1987)

Without Me you will live like the world, with Me you will live like in Heaven; without Me your traits will become those of the world, but with Me your traits will be Mine; remain in Me; rooted in Me, never neglect your gift, have Me as first and grant Me your time. (May 20, 1994)

Chapter Sixteen

Meeting God in Prayer

J.N.: Every Christian, every person who practices a religion, knows that we can meet God in prayer; that this way is always at our disposal, even if in everyday life we have, more often than not, a tendency to forget it. I would like to ask you a few questions about prayer and the difficulties we have in praying. The first is about purification, entering into a state of prayer. We meet people who are complete nonbelievers, who say they do not encounter God, that they cannot manage to meet God. When they try praying, they find only boredom and silence. In the beginning, we must give them some encouragement and explain to them the origin of this aridity of the heart.

V.:   The key to meeting God is truly prayer. First, we must put our life in order. God is very merciful. He does not wait for us to be perfect before He speaks to us; He does not wait for us to become saints. He takes us as we are on earth now. He gives us graces. He says: "Come as you are! With all your wretchedness. And I will forgive you. But take a step!" Some people wait for everything to happen miraculously. I know many who come to me and say: "Please! I do not get any answer, but pray for me." They don't do anything but they should ask themselves if they are doing all that is possible. In a word, we must decide for God. If we do not decide for God, we do not progress in sincerity, because God looks at the heart. If we haven't sincerity of heart and we only repeat words, we never progress. We will never encounter

God. A young person told me: "But I do not know how to pray. I have never prayed. So what should I do?" I replied: "Can you talk to your best friend?" He told me: "Of course!" So I told him: "God is your best friend. You only have to talk to Him. Converse with Him. It's simple." He asked me: "That's all?" I answered: "Yes. You will talk as you talk to your best friend. You tell Him everything. If you have a backache, you start by telling this. You talk with God and that conversation becomes a prayer because it goes toward God."

J.N.: The first step.

V.: Then there's the purification. We must really repent. The fruit of repentance sets in motion many spiritual impulses, especially love. Contact with God, God's blessings. If we do not forgive, if we do not ask God's forgiveness, if we do not reconcile with God and our neighbor, if we do not forgive our neighbor the wrongs he has done to us, we cannot receive God's blessings.

J.N.: Is a formal step, such as confession, required besides repentance of the heart?

V.: Yes. This is important. Confession is very important. In my ignorance, I was opposed to it in the beginning. I had to be brought to it little by little. I was very rebellious. I was quite embarrassed when the Lord told me: "You have to confess." I was wondering why I had to go to a priest since I had a direct contact with God and could confess directly. He told me: "You can confess to me as you wish, every day even, but it is a law I have given. I would like you to confess to a priest so he can give you absolution." In spite of my resistance I agreed because the Lord asked it with such insistence. He was angry because I had protested. As I was writing He took the pencil away from me and threw it to the other side of the room. And He told me: "Do you realize it is I who am talking to you?" Well then I was a little afraid and I said: "All right!"

154

J.N.: The Orthodox Church also has confession?
V.: Yes.

J.N.: So, before your conversion, you could have gone to confession in an Orthodox Church. Did you ever go?
V.: No.

J.N.: Never?
V.: Never.

J.N.: So your very first confession was after your conversion. Very early or after a few months?
V.: After a few weeks.

J.N.: After a few weeks and making use of this Catholic seminary on the other side of the street.
V.: Yes. Many people tell me:

But I haven't done anything serious. I have a very honest family life. I love my husband, my children, besides I haven't stolen, or killed, so why should I confess? I am charitable; I give a lot of money to the poor, so why should I confess? What is there to confess?

Then I reply; "Only because of what you've said, it's already enough to have to go to confession. Because you think you are perfect." When we go to confession, we must first ask ourselves if we have prayed enough, if we have kept the First Commandment? To love God. Do we love God as He wants us to? We are never perfect and we must confess anyhow for not having respected the First Commandment.

J.N.: A third step, after repentance and confession, is penance. What can you say about either the penances that are given to us, or those we impose on ourselves such as fasting, prayers, and alms?
V.: Penance can be fasting because it amounts to mortifying

the senses. It is difficult to understand that at first, but once we begin, we experience interior satisfaction. You cannot do it without noticing something. There are other penances that God imposes on us Himself. To obtain sanctification, for the sick, those who are dying a slow death from a serious disease and who endure suffering, this is purification. They are going through purification. It is the end of their life, and at the last moment, God purifies the soul. Suffering purifies the soul.

J.N.: Do you know Louis XIV's last words? He suffered a rather long agony that lasted many days, and had asked for his great-grandson who was to succeed him as Louis XV. Of course the child asked him if he suffered greatly. And Louis XIV replied: "I suffer greatly but I would like to suffer even more to repair all that I have done." Evidently, he had many sins to be forgiven.

V.: There is the story about St. Teresa of Avila who had fallen off her donkey into an icy stream. Wet and ice cold she called out to Him: "Why are You treating me this way?" The Lord answered: "That is the way I treat My friends." And Teresa then said: "No wonder You have so few friends if you treat them like this." During a certain period I was suffering so much I told Him the same thing, I told Him: "Allow me to take the words of Saint Teresa, because I cannot keep silent, I must tell You." He didn't say anything then, He gave me a message and, at the end, while He made as if He were leaving He said: "Concerning your remark, if you knew how much you obtain through suffering, you would beg Me on your knees to have more to bear."

J.N.: Another moment in prayer is dryness, the absolute dryness that all monks, all nuns encounter. The night of the soul.

V.: Everybody goes through this period that can last for a very long time, years sometimes, but after this period there is always a light that shines stronger than before. God likes to be sought after in that way. One day someone came to tell me: "You know, today I feel as cold as stone. Only yesterday I was burning with love for God and full of joy. And now I am totally cold, what is going on?" And Jesus tells us: "I take the flame from your heart to light up other hearts which are cold and then I return and give it back to you."

J.N.: It's a nice image. They say moreover that St. Teresa suffered for about fifteen years from absolute night. I would now like to talk about the material conditions for prayer. Can we pray while doing anything or should we, to be well prepared, arrange a little prayer room such as the one you have, or go into a church, or stay in darkness or in silence?

V.: We can choose. A church is an appropriate place to receive the holy sacraments; there is a prayerful atmosphere inside. But a church is not the only place for praying. Some people go to church, they come out of the church and then they leave God in the church until the following week. That is not a life of prayer. God should be in our life constantly. It is worthwhile to set up a little prayer room at home, like the one I have, for daily prayer. Still we must keep God constantly in mind, in our soul. And even if I must cook, my prayer cannot stop.

J.N.: It is a continuous prayer?

V.: Contemplative prayer does not need words. It is the prayer of silence, if you wish. Because a prayer of the heart, without words, and the thirst of our soul for God are prayers, it is adoration from the heart toward God who is there, before us, always present. But the Lord also likes very much for us to converse with Him. This spontaneous prayer of the heart pleases God very much, because He told me so. And also prayers like the rosary, for example, because it is meditation. There are many prayers. It is a contact with God; it is the first contact. Some people ask me:

"How do we contact God?" The first step to encounter God is prayer.

J.N.: Can we pray in every circumstance? Or are there activities that prevent us from praying?

V.: Yes, for example when we are watching a football game on television. I will have many football fans against me after this. But it's the first example that came to my mind. You must understand that our life becomes a constant prayer if we live in the love of God. We must never forget to put God first.

J.N.: I would quite agree with that example. Any others?

V.: If we are talking business in an office we are not talking about God. Money is not an obstacle in itself, but the attention we are giving it in a business discussion. But it is also possible to have this discussion in the love of God.

J.N.: Another example: can we pray to God in a nightclub?

V.: No. God is not particularly present in nightclubs. But if someone is profoundly unhappy and cries to God, even if he is hanging around in a nightclub, because of a great unhappiness in his life, he will be heard, because God lives in us.

J.N.: Extreme noise, such as the music the young listen to, can we pray while listening to that?

V.: No, that is out. The purpose of this music is precisely to stir them up.

J.N.: Alcohol?

V.: No, because alcoholism is a demon.

J.N.: May I tell you a story that you may have already heard; it is about a Dominican who asks the pope: "May I smoke while praying?" The pope says: "No." Then comes a Jesuit who asks: "May I pray while smoking?" And the pope replies: "Yes."

V.: Fortunately, it's only an anecdote.

J.N.: An apt reply. Do you pray before meals at home?

V.: Yes. I never blessed food before because I hadn't been taught. The Lord wanted to teach me to pray, to thank Him for the meal He is giving us. He didn't ask me directly, explicitly in a message. But He appeared to me while I was preparing lunch for myself. I was sitting down eating quietly and I saw Him. He was looking at me. And I was a little embarrassed because my mouth was full. He looked at me and then, after a few moments, He asked me: "Is it good?" I replied: "Yes Lord." I didn't know what to do because I was ill at ease. He asked me: "Don't you want me to bless it?" And I understood. He stayed to the end. He didn't say another word. He stayed until I had finished and I understood what He was waiting for. He wanted me to thank Him at the end of the meal.

J.N.: What role can beauty play in the spirit of prayer, in making praying easier? I am thinking about music, works of art, paintings, sculptures, stained glass, architecture, religious or not, so long as it is beautiful. Is it necessary and useful?

V.: You mean art?

J.N.: Art, yes.

V.: I will tell you a story about art. God the Father asked me in a message: "Have you got anything to give Me?" And He added right away: "But then, whatever you will give me that is good, comes from Me." I asked Him: "Do you mean that I do not have anything good by myself to give You?" He said: "No, nothing." I thought for a moment and said: "I know what I must do to please You which would be good and would come from me. I'll paint an icon and give it to You, offer it to the church." He told me: "The gift of art, Vassula, also comes from Me."

J.N.: In the circumstances there is a perfect identification. Are there forms of art that are satanic?

V.: Of course such forms of art exist because Satan exists.

J.N.: I mean forms of art that bring people to worship Satan and particularly pervert them.

V.: Yes of course there are.

J.N.: Is there music that seems to be played by or for the devil?

V.: Certain kinds of music contain subliminal messages. There are audiocassettes. I didn't know these existed. A priest explained to me what subliminal messages were. There was even a case in the United States where parents have accused a band of having pushed their son to suicide.

J.N.: Outside of subliminal messages that might be included in a piece of music, are there, among musicians, some who lead to God and some who lead away from God? Personally, I think that Johann Sebastian Bach takes us by the hand and leads us to God without any doubt. With others, Beethoven for example, it is not clear where they lead me. There are musicians who lead me to despair, who would lead me to despair if I listened to them, for example, Tchaikovsky.

V.: Really? When I hear the latest style of music, rap for example, I can't listen even three seconds. It pains me to my soul; it's awful. People will say I'm old-fashioned, perhaps. But I see the reactions of the young. They become violent, they start to be aggressive. It's Satan's trademark.

J.N.: Does that mean you are opposed to the kind of music the young like?

V.: No, not at all. I'm not interested only in classical music and in traditional liturgical music. I appreciate the choirs in the churches of young people who are accompanied by the guitar. Their songs are not old-fashioned at all; they are rather light and gay and are a witness to the joy of God. When I travel through countries in Africa and Asia I like it when there are traditional dances. It's organized to celebrate the glory of God, and I feel like joining in. My angel did not keep me from appreciating popular music but he introduced me to classical music that I didn't understand before my conversion.

J.N.: Do you advise people to make, from time to time, what is called a retreat? To remove oneself from the ordinary world, take three days, a week?

V.: Absolutely. We must choose a suitable retreat. Some retreats are fruitless if they are not well prepared. Maybe we should choose retreats where you spend one week without talking in order to talk only to God. Some people are literally panic-stricken at this thought. When the week is over they feel good. It's like an interior cleansing. We become more clear-minded, able to understand God and be with God at the same time. I think it is very beautiful that we can withdraw from time to time. Of course it's not easy to find silence when you are living in a city. For those who have the chance to go away and be in touch with nature and heaven, it is advisable. And then talk to God.

J.N.: Could you say a word about the respective merits of personal prayer and communal prayer? What is the benefit of communal prayer versus personal prayer?

V.: Jesus said: "When two or three gather in My name, I will be among you." It does not mean that He is not going to listen to you if you are alone, but that the sharing of prayer adds strength. And strength brings the power of the Holy Spirit.

J.N.: Could you say something about religious life? For some people the question arises. After having met God, do I remain in the world, getting married, and having children, or do I choose religious life?

V.:   One cannot become a priest or a religious if he has not received a call from God. Without a specific calling (vocation) one should stay in the world. We can be apostles in the lay world. I received a prediction that, at the end of times, there will be many apostles. We can witness. The pope, for one, very much encourages lay people to be witnesses to God's love. We can through our way of life be an example and a witness to others. Marriage is a sacrament.

J.N.:   Have you ever, let's say when you were twenty, told yourself: "I should seriously consider the possibility of entering a convent?" Never before your conversion? And after?

V.:   When you are converted as I have been, all of a sudden, you are profoundly shaken. At that moment you discover God. He is so near then, because He smiles at you and you feel Him so strongly. God begins to teach you detachment, but always respecting your freedom. You must consent to detach from the world, from things, and then from all frivolous attachments. Detachment proceeds up to the point where you are detached from your own self. At that stage, you wish you were in heaven. In *True Life in God* there is a passage which says: "Although you will still be among men, your mind will be in heaven; and although your body will be moving among men, your soul and mind will be as an angel's, walking in the Courts of Our Kingdom, walking among angels." It is this detachment that is very difficult, because you realize that God will not call you to heaven right away and you have to go on as you are on earth, encumbered with all those things from which you have been detached. So I cried to Him, I said: "Why have You done this? Why have You detached me to this extent and then left me here?" But then He helps you to go on while remaining detached. I know many who have been through this stage. I give them a lot of encouragement, I tell them: "It doesn't matter. You still have some painful days ahead. You will overcome all this." But it is still a difficult stage to go through.

J.N.: Of course, if you remain in your present circumstances it is because you have a family.

V.: Yes, it is my family but also the family of brothers and sisters in the world to whom I must bear witness. The Lord will not let me go. He told me He would not let me leave this world if I have not completed my mission. And my mission is twofold; the family and the communication of the messages. In the past, before my conversion, I never bothered to find out if my soul pleased my Creator. It was more important for me to look good and to shine in the eyes of the world. Now, since my conversion, I have seen how futile beauty and exterior wealth are, and after meeting God I was hungry for being with Him alone. One single meeting face to Face with God was enough to give me this longing to abandon everything for His sake.

Now I do not accumulate "treasures" anymore. Although my husband has a good salary, I am no longer preoccupied with constantly buying clothes and jewels just for the pleasure of buying as I used to. The beauty of a person is within. I am not neglecting myself, however, but now I buy only what I really need. Many people, who do not have God in their life, try continually to collect money or things, such as the latest model stereo, the latest model car, the latest television set. Often their conversation deals only with trivial matters. They long to fill their emptiness. Their soul is thirsty for God, but they are not aware of it, and so, to fill their emptiness they fill their soul with earthly treasures, and since these never satisfy them they keep on looking for more. They can spend their entire life like this, searching, without finding God, while God is **everything**. And yet, God never ceases calling out to us and knocking at the door of our hearts.

J.N.: Let's suppose that, through an unfortunate combination of circumstances you should lose your husband and children and find yourself alone in the world.

V.: God decides on life or death, but as long as my mission is not completed the Lord will not take me. He knows the day and the hour. As for myself, I cannot say. The charism will last until the end of my life. When I ask Him: "When will it be over?" He answers: "When this work is well-established."

J.N.: So, until the end of your life you will play the role of a traveling missionary. That's it.

V.: A witness.

J.N.: And to be a witness. But you have no inclination to go into a convent, Catholic or Orthodox, or a charismatic community that you would create?

V.: No, that is, I will not do anything by myself that God has not asked me to do.

J.N.: And He does not tell you to do anything like that?

V.: He never told me. At first, I did not know what God's intentions were, and He didn't reveal them to me because He wanted me to be frank. It was beautiful, because He wanted me to argue with Him, to open my heart, to trust Him, so I was afraid. In my ignorance, at first, I was telling myself: "There is a call from God. It's not for nothing. He wants something from me. And surely He wants to call me to a convent, and leave my whole family to become a Carmelite." The Lord knew I had that question in mind. He wanted me to speak out to Him. And He told me: "I would like you to live holy." And I said to myself: "There, He is going to ask me to drop my family." And I was afraid. He asked me: "Why are you afraid?" I replied: "No. Nothing at all." I wanted to escape, but it didn't work. For two days He didn't stop saying: "Tell me what is in your heart. Why are you afraid of Me?" And finally I asked Him: "Would you like me to be frank?"

J.N.: The question is rather piquant.

V.: He told me: "Yes, My daughter." And then I told Him: "I don't really want to be a nun." He said: "I never asked you to become a nun. I have asked you for your heart."

J.N.: You have reported that, according to the messages, your charism will last until this institution is well-established.

V.: Yes.

J.N.: Does that mean that this work would eventually develop into a community of living?

V.: I do not know the future. Up to now, I have not received any such sign. But I perceive, nevertheless, tendencies toward a community organized more like a retreat house, if you will, with the retreat based on the Trinitarian spirituality of *True Life in God.* In Rhodes, where we go every summer, there are more and more people coming from everywhere. They come when they know I am there for two months. Then we have a retreat and a pilgrimage at the same time. We visit Patmos, we visit the islands where there are monasteries, and I see more and more people joining us. We pray every day. And finally it's like a retreat. And I say to the Lord: "If you want us to have something, you have to speak more clearly."

J.N.: So, it is a possibility?

V.: A possibility, yes.

CHAPTER SEVENTEEN

Concluding Observations

Vassula's charism unfolds essentially in three dimensions: teaching that prayer is the means to meet God; showing that the role of the laity can and must become more important than it is now in the churches; bringing about the unity of Christians at the grass roots level without waiting for an agreement at the summit. A threefold and formidable message because it goes against the spirit of the world, which is made up of indifference, apostasy, entertainment, and politically correct and abysmally hollow discourse. Such is the essence of the message that its opponents often try to drown in disputes over details.

We should not omit, however, to point out that participants in prayer groups led by Vassula regularly report spectacular phenomena: sometimes the sun turns in a spinning motion as it did in Fatima; sometimes Jesus' face is superimposed over Vassula's; sometimes Vassula experiences the sufferings of the Passion; occasionally, miraculous cures are reported. Not to mention these would be incomplete and one-sided. I mention it only briefly because it does not seem to be essential to the charismatic phenomenon that Vassula represents. Those exceptional events replicate episodes reported within the context of other apparitions. Some people may brush them aside, considering them not to be purely objective, while others may consider them as fabrications by witnesses always on the lookout for supernatural signs. A few may be interested in them in a spirit of sensationalism which is quite out of place here. We will not refer to this again, since the emphasis is not there.

Vassula's charismatic phenomenon includes characteristics that are much more essential: a life of prayer turned toward others; messages faithful to the teachings of Scripture and Tradition; a call to conversion in times of great apostasy; crowds responding to that call; an unbending fidelity to the pope; and a call for unity of the churches. Vassula's message amounts to this: it is always possible to encounter God directly through prayer. This in itself is neither revolutionary nor extravagant. Compared to this message, limpid in its ordinariness, the controversies about whether the phenomenon is supernatural or not, seem ridiculous. Purely formalistic criticisms on questions of theology become wearisome. Just as, during the trial of Joan of Arc, an entire faculty of theology relentlessly harassed a poor ignorant and illiterate peasant girl, trying to trap her with theoretical and speculative statements. If Jesus Himself returned to earth, would He not fail the exams in a theological faculty?

As I stated at the very beginning, I will avoid making any declaration as to whether Vassula's revelations are supernatural or not. There is no scientific method for distinguishing between what is natural and what is supernatural. My scientific training does not give me any extra authority. Any affirmation on that matter belongs to subjective evaluation. Supposing that such a method existed, to apply it would be presumption on my part; I have no training in ascetical and mystical theology; I hold no mandate from my church; I respect the readers who are quite able to form an opinion by themselves.

In any case, it seems premature to pass judgment on a person while that person is still living. Just as we cannot evaluate a book on the basis of a few quotations out of context, it is dangerous to judge a person until she has produced the totality of her work, and we have had the time to read it with a clear mind after all controversies have died down. The Galileo and Darwin affairs are there to teach us the necessity of caution before pronouncing hasty judgments which may be disastrous in the long run and harmful to the credibility of the church.

This policy of prudence was ignored when warnings were issued against Vassula with such urgency. The local Catholic Church was unable to tolerate, within its borders, a woman who communicated private revelations to the faithful. To a certain extent, the contents of the revelations and the conversions recorded in the wake of Vassula's testimony were of no importance. The obviously positive aspects of her action simply complicated the drafting of the warnings that were based on other motives. It was as if the charism, acceptable in theory, becomes inadmissible when it actually occurs.

The sudden appearance of a "parallel magisterium" is dreaded by an ecclesiastical bureaucracy. The frailty of this institution, its desertion by the faithful, its difficulties in recruiting clergy, the questioning of moral theology, the struggle to formulate answers to serious problems of society, its internal contestation by adventurous theologians or fundamentalists loyal to an embarrassing past, all of that does not predispose it to heed prophets whose providential function consists in destabilizing institutions. The rigidity of an organization does not reveal its strength but its frailty. To use a technical metaphor, it is not made of steel but of cast iron, a material that resists very well under pressure but breaks if we try to bend it. The Catholic Church is not flexible, undoubtedly because her intrinsic function consists in not bending to external pressures.

When Joan of Arc went up at the stake in Rouen, after an ecclesiastical tribunal had unanimously condemned her, she did so trembling, wondering whether she was not a victim of illusion, in childish terror of the suffering she was to endure. But it seemed impossible to her not to remain faithful to the voices she was hearing: better to sacrifice her life than betray what had given meaning to her life. She was a martyr, that is, a witness of faith before men whose function was precisely to rationalize that faith. She imitated Jesus in what was the most intolerable of His Passion, condemnation by the ministers of God. The character of the prophet lies in his capacity to be as inflexible as a church, but alone against all, to witness that only God gives him the strength to resist men.

Vassula told me laughingly that she would have been burned as a witch had she lived a few centuries earlier. Listening to her, it seemed to me that she belongs to that breed which is willing to be burnt at the stake. Nothing will stop a movement animated by persons of that sort. Persecutions, whether mild or violent, act as a spur and gather audiences that are more and more convinced. Of course, it is a characteristic to be found at the very core of Christianity, doubtless because it is founded on the proclamation of the ignominious death of the Son of God and His scandalous Resurrection. What are we to do to maintain order, decency, and discipline before such provocations, when God Himself is their author?

Thus, both supporters and opponents of Vassula play their role in the psychodrama that constitutes the spiritual source of our civilization. Antigone before Creon, Socrates before the Areopagus, Jesus before the Sanhedrin, Joan of Arc before Bishop Cauchon, Galileo before the Holy Office, Dreyfus before the French Army, Charles de Gaulle before Philippe Pétain,

Solzhenitsyn before the KGB. To play out that psychodrama, each one of the protagonists must act his role well, following his particular logic to its conclusion. A country cannot be governed without a Creon at its head, but it is better governed if there is an Antigone who stands up to him.

It is the same with the Catholic Church that fascinates and irritates us through these two inseparable aspects of her life. In the universal Church founded by Jesus, there is a visible part, the churches, like the visible tip of an iceberg. Despite the danger of confusing the means with the end, we cannot do without an organization which collects money, keeps up buildings, organizes catechism, designates ordained ministers, puts up posters, publishes books of prayers and hymns; the whole visible church is a terribly human enterprise with all the deficiencies that are to be expected.

In the universal Church there are also prophets, seers, and mystics—persons totally immersed in God, who for the most part are invisible but who cause the visible tip of the iceberg to emerge by a hidden upward push.

Vassula fully acknowledges the visible church which she needs, not only to give her the means for her apostolate but also as a place for praying and which dispenses the Sacraments. Since the visible church does not know whether Vassula belongs to the invisible church—the invisible is not immediately obvious—it hesitates and refuses, at least for the time being, to support her action, without condemning her completely, however. Each one of the partners in the psychodrama takes the other into consideration and plays his role soberly. Fortunately, we have reached a point in history where we no longer erect stakes for burning.

In the end, if Vassula dies after a lifetime of prayer, if she brings about lasting conversions through her action, if what we call miracles occur, we cannot rule out the possibility that she may be canonized, that is, acknowledged, reclaimed, restored by the visible church. By definition, the latter can reasonably canonize only saints that are already dead. Introducing the invisible into the visible, recognizing the charism of the mystics, asking them to lead devotions, all that would cause the visible church to implode. Besides, saints refuse while they are living to be involved in the ecclesiastical structure. They know instinctively the risks they would run.

If Jesus had become a doctor of the law in the synagogue and had been recognized as a distinguished rabbi, we would have good reasons to doubt He was the Son of God. He had to be put to death and rise again so we would believe in His Divinity. Such is the paradox lying at the very heart of our faith. A Christian Church must, in a same movement, organize itself and accept being disorganized by the inrush of the divine disorder that is contrary to the order men desire. At the beginning of the Church, Saint Paul said that the folly of God surpasses the wisdom of men. That paradox is not a contradiction as yet unresolved, but a creative tension that men cannot fully comprehend.

The least we can say about Vassula is that she fulfills the paradoxical conditions specific to prophets: a life of prayer, giving priority to one's duty over contemplation, absence of ostentation, lack of previous theological or simply religious formation, disinterestedness, the feeling of having to communicate a message and of being a simple instrument, soundness of answers to classical pitfalls, refusal to enter into controversy in the face of attacks, vigorous calls for the unity of the churches, unshakable fidelity to the pope. And then what is difficult to express in words: approachability, kindness, serenity, the kind of regal calm of a woman certain of the love of God which nothing can take from her.

APPENDIX

A Collection of Prayers
Recommended by Vassula

Jesus said to me: "Go out to the nations and teach them to pray to the Father this prayer:"

Father all Merciful, let those who hear and hear again yet never understand, hear Your Voice this time and understand that it is You the Holy of Holies.

Open the eyes of those who see and see, yet never perceive, to see with their eyes this time, Your Holy Face and Your Glory. Place Your Finger on their heart so that their heart may open and understand Your Faithfulness.

I pray and ask You all these things, Righteous Father so that all the nations be converted and be healed through the Wounds of Your Beloved Son, Jesus Christ. Amen.

The Rosary
After the first three Hail Marys, we say the Prayer to St. Michael composed by Pope Leo XIII:

St. Michael the Archangel, defend us in the day of battle, be our safeguard against the wickedness and snares of the devil! May God rebuke him, we humbly pray, and do thou O Prince of the Heavenly Host, by the Power of God, cast into Hell, Satan and all the other evil spirits who prowl through the world seeking the ruin of souls! Amen.

And the Memorare of St. Bernard:
Remember, O most gracious Virgin Mary that never was it known that anyone who fled to thy protection, implored thy help or sought thy intercession, was left unaided. Inspired by this confidence, I fly unto them. O Virgin of Virgins my Mother! To thee do I come, before thee

I stand, sinful and sorrowful. O Mother of the Word Incarnate! Despise not my petitions but in thy mercy hear and answer me. Amen.

After every decade of the rosary, we pray the prayer given at Fatima: "O My Jesus, forgive us our sins, save us from the fires of hell, and lead all souls to heaven, especially those in most need of Your Mercy. Amen."

Then we say the prayer that Jesus asked us to pray after every decade (August 8, 1993, in *True Life in God*): "Jesus, my only Love, I pray for those whom You love but know not how to love You; may they be purified and healed so that they too be exempt from all evil. Amen."

Then at the end of the Rosary, we say the Salve Regina:

Salve Regina, Mater Misericordiae, Vita, dulcedo et spes nostra salve. Ad Te clamamus, exsules, filii Hevae. At Te suspiramus, gementes et flentes, in hac lacrimarum valle. Eia ergo, Advocata nostra, illos tuos misericordes oculos ad nos converte. Et Jesus benefictum fructum ventris tui, nobis post hoc exilium ostende. O Clemens, o pia, o dulcis Virgo Maria.

Hymns

We sing a hymn or two.

Prayer to the Holy Spirit

We stand and pray, invoking the Holy Spirit with a prayer from the Byzantine Liturgy:

O Heavenly King, Paraclete, Spirit of Truth, Omnipresent and in all; the Treasure of the simple in spirit and the Given of Life, come and pitch Your tent inside us and cleanse us from any stain and save our soul, O most Pure. Amen.

Or the

Veni Creator:

Come, Holy Ghost, Creator, come. From thy bright heavenly throne! Come, take possession of our souls, And make them all Thine Own! Thou who art called the Paraclete, Best gift of God above, The Living Spring, The Living Fire, Sweet Unction, and True Love! Thou who are sevenfold in Thy grace, Finger of God's right hand, His Promise, teaching little ones To speak and understand! O guide our minds with Thy blest light, With love our hearts inflame, And with Thy strength, which ne'er decays, Confirm our mortal frame. Far from us drive our hellish foe, True peace unto us bring, And through all perils guide us safe Beneath Thy sacred wing. Through Thee may we the Father know, Through Thee the Eternal Son, And Thee the Spirit of them both— Thrice blessed Three in One. Now to the Father, and the Son, Who rose from death, be glory given, With Thee, O holy Comforter, Henceforth by all in earth and heaven. Amen.

Prayer from the Heart

While standing, we may offer God prayers from the heart. Here are some examples of prayers of intercession:

Jesus said: "I have come that you may have life and have it to the full." Let us pray that all people will come to Jesus who is True Life in God. (Response: *Lord hear us.)*

Jesus said: "I am the Light of the world. Whoever follows Me will have the light of life and never walk in darkness." Let us pray for all those who are broken and wounded and walking in darkness that they will follow Jesus, who is True Life in God. *(Lord hear us.)*

Jesus said to Simon and Andrew as they were fishing: "Come, follow Me and I will make you fishers of men." Let us pray for all clergy and religious that they will follow Jesus, who is the True Life in God. *(Lord hear us.)*

Jesus said: "I am the Resurrection." Let us pray for those who are still away from Jesus and who ceased to be spiritually alive, that they too may be liberated and resurrected to live a True Life in God. *(Lord hear us.)*

Hymn or Prayer of Praise

We praise the Lord either by singing or saying any prayer. Here is one that was inspired by the Holy Spirit to Vassula (November 10, 1995):

Glory be to God in the highest heaven. Glory be to Him who lifted my soul from the entrails of this earth. Glory be to the Light thrice Holy in whose power all things came to be. Glory be to God, Invincible, Incomparable in His Authority; Glory be to the Immortal One in whom we find immortality; May Your Breath, Most Holy One, which is pure emanation of Your Glory, enliven us, renewing us into one glorious Body. Amen.

Meditations

We pray and ask Our Lord to give us a message from the Holy Bible first, then from one of the books of True Life in God. *We open at random because we know God is with us and hears us. We read aloud the two messages and meditate upon them for a while.*

Healing Service

We may then have a healing service while asking God to grant us His gifts from the Holy Spirit. Hymns can be sung while people are prayed over, or the rosary could be prayed.

Consecration to the Sacred Heart

We conclude with the Consecration Prayer to the Sacred Heart of Jesus. (Prayer given on January 26, 1992.)

Sacred Heart of Jesus, come and invade me completely so that my motives will be Your Motives, my desires Your Desires, my words Your Words, my thoughts Your Thoughts. Then allow me to creep in the deepest place of Your Sacred Heart. Annihilate me altogether. I, [your name], shall worship Your Sacred Heart from the core of mine. I promise to serve Your Sacred Heart with a fire inside me. I shall, with zeal, serve You more fervently than before. I am weak but I know that Your Strength shall sustain me. Do not allow me to lose sight of You, nor allow my heart to flutter elsewhere. I, [your name], will look for Your Sacred Heart alone and desire You alone.

Sacred Heart of Jesus, make me dislike all that is contrary to Your Holiness and to Your Will. Sift me through and through and make sure that not one rival remains within me. From today, tighten the bonds of Love with which you have enlaced me and make my soul thirst for You and my heart sick with love for You.

Sacred Heart of Jesus, do not wait, come and consume my whole being with the Flames of Your ardent Love. Whatever I do from now on, will be done merely for Your Interests and Your Glory and nothing for me. I, [your name], consecrate my life for you and from today am willing to be the slave of Your Love, the victim of Your Burning Desires and of Your Passion, the benefit of Your Church, and the toy of Your Soul. Make my traits resemble those of Your Crucifixion through the bitterness I will encounter in the deafness of souls and to see them fall. Give my soul its fill.

Sacred Heart of Jesus, do not spare me from Your Cross, like the Father had not spared You. Arrest my eyes, my thoughts and my desires to be captives of Your Sacred Heart. Unworthy I am and I deserve nothing, but help me to live my act of consecration by being loyal, invoking Your Holy Name untiringly. Make my spirit repulse all that is not You.

Sacred Heart of Jesus, make my soul bear more than ever before, the Marks of Your Body for the conversion of souls. I, [your name], voluntarily submit my will to Your Will, now and forever. Amen.

Biography of Jacques Neirynck

a) Born in 1931 in Brussels, he has dual citizenship, Swiss and French. Married and the father of five children, he received a bachelor's degree in electrical engineering from the Catholic University of Louvain in 1954 and a Ph.D. in applied sciences in 1958.

b) From 1954 to 1957, he worked as an engineer for the Foraky Company in the charcoal mines of Hainaut.

c) From 1957 to 1963, he was assistant professor, then professor at the University of Lovanium, in Kinshasa, Zaire. He created a course on the theory of electronic circuits.

d) From 1963 to 1972, he was team leader and assistant director of the research laboratory MBLE of Philips in Brussels. Starting in 1970, he became technical director of the team in charge of circuit simulation in the framework of integrated circuit design for all of the Philips Group.

e) From 1967 to 1972, he served as professor extraordinary at L'Université Catholique de Louvain where he taught circuit theory.

f) In 1972, he joined l'Ecole Polytechnique Federale de Lausanne as professor where he directed the Department of Circuits and Systems. In 1996 he was nominated honorary teacher.

g) Since 1963, he was engaged in the consumerism movement in France, Belgium, and Switzerland as editor of the magazine *"Test-Achats"* and *"Que Choisir."* He took part in numerous radio and TV programs, particularly one titled "A Bon Entendeur" at Romand Swiss Television for which he was a technical consultant from 1976 to1986. He also participated in the Romand Swiss radio program called "Cinq sur Cinq."

h) In October 1999, he was elected national counselor on PDC electoral list of the Canton de Vaud. He still is a member of the two parliamentary commissions on science, education, culture and transportation, and telecommunications.

i) In 1999, he was elected member of the Swiss Federal Parliament where he is particularly in charge of the commissions for education and communications.

Distinctions

In 1959 he received a Fellowship from the Belgian American Educational Foundation.

In 1981, the Institute of Electrical and Electronics Engineers (IEEE) granted him the title of Fellow, its highest distinction.

In 1986, he received the Denzler Prize for the publication of the *Traité d'Eléctricité*.

In 1994, the Institute of Electrical and Electronics Engineers (IEEE) granted him the Major Educational Innovation Distinction Award for the creation of the institute Eurécom.

In 1995, he received the Library and Religious Literature Prize, and in 1996 the Award Charles Oulmont from Fondation de France for his novel *Le Manuscrit du Saint Sépulcre*.

Functions

a) Head of the Electricity Department of the EPFL in 1978, then again from 1983 to 1985. Founded in 1991 and presided over the Department of System and Communication Engineers of the EPFL until 1996. He also presided over the Scientific Council of Eurécom from 1991 to 1992, and was member of the assembly of the "GIE Institut Eurécom" from 1991–1996.

b) Vice-president, then president, of the IEEE Switzerland section from 1981–1982 and 1983–1984. He also was vice-president of the Circuits and Systems Society (New York) from 1987 to 1990.

c) Associate editor of the *Franklin Institute Journal* from 1970 to 1996, member of the editorial board of the *International Journal of Circuit Theory and Application* (London) from 1972 to 1997, as well as member of the Editorial Board of the *Journal of Circuits, Systems, and Computers* (Singapore) from 1985–1997. Member of the Comité des Anales des Telecommunications since 1986, he was president of the same from 1992–1997.

d) Founded the Conseil de Fondation des Presses Polytechniques et Universitaires Romandes (Lausanne) in 1980 and presided over it from 1980 to 1992. He also created the Librairie Polytechnique, S.A. (Lausanne) in 1987, and managed it from 1987 to 1991.

e) Member of the Managing Council of the Institut de Génie Electrique of the Paul Sabatier University (Toulouse) from 1986 to 1990.

f) Administrator of Conseur (Luxembourg), an agency for European consumer protection (France, Belgium, Italy, Portugal, and Spain) until 1999. He also presided over *Test Achats* (Brussels) from 1968 to 1974.

g) Member of the Council of the Foundation Odier (Geneva) and "L'homme et le Temps" (la Chaux de Fond) since 1997.

Bibliography

Author of hundreds of articles in scientific publications, which include:

a) *"Analyse des Circuits Linéaires"* (with René Boite) (Gordon and Breach, Paris, 1971).

b) *"Théorie des Réseaux de Kirchhoff"* (with René Boite) (Georgi, St-Saphorin, 1976), Spanish translation, *"Teoria de las redes de Kirchhoff"* (Limusa, Mexico).

c) *"Filtres électriques"* (with Martin Hasler) (Georgi, St-Saphorin, 1981), English translation, "Electric Filters" (Artech, Dedham).

d) *"Circuits non Lineaires"* (with Martin Hasler) (Press Polytechniques Romandes, Lausanne, 1985). English translation, "Nonlinear Circuits" (Artech, Dedham). Editor-in-chief of the redaction of *Traité d'Electricité,* published between 1976 and 1986, a 22-volume collection presenting a systematic summary of electrical techniques.

He has authored hundreds of publications of general interest, which include:

a) *Le Consommateur Averti* (Favre, Lausanne, 1978).

b) *Le Huitienme Jour de la Creation* (Presses Polytechniques Romandes, Lausanne, 1986). German translation, *Der Gottliche Ingenieur* (Expert Verlag, Sindelfingen).

c) *Premiere Epitre aux Techniciens* (with Philipe Baud). (Presses Polytechniques et Universitaires Romandes, Lausanne, 1990).

d) *L'enigme Vassula* Vassula (Favre, Lausanne, 2000). Translation in German and Japanese.

e) *Tout Savoir sur le Genie Genetique* (Favre, Lausanne, 1998).

f) *Peut-on Vivre avec l'Islam?* (Favre, Lausanne, 1999). Italian translation.

g) *Swissmetro* (Favre, Lausanne, 2000).

And some novels:

a) *Le Manuscrit du Saint-Sepulcre* (cerf, Paris, 1994). Translation in German (Rowohlt, Reinbeck), Spanish (PPC, Madrid), Portuguese

(Noticias, Lisbonne), Italian (Piemme, Monferrato Casale).
b) *Le Siege de Bruxelles* (Desclée de Brouwer, Paris, 1996).
c) *Les Cendres de Superphenix* (Desclée de Brouwer, Paris, 1997).
d) *L'Ange dans le Placard* (Desclée de Brouwer, Paris, 1999).

Address:

E-mail: jacques.neirynck@epfl.ch

Interview of
Jacques Nierynch, May 1997

"Let Vassula—Joan of Arc of modern times—speak!"

(An interview by Anna Lietti; published and copyrighted by
Le Nouveau Quotidien, Geneva, Switzerland, Friday, May 16, 1997)

The professor from Lausanne has turned his attention on the case of the woman who says she writes under God's dictation. One would have expected a scientific study. We have just a series of interviews. Is it really reasonable?

Five hundred copies sold on the first day of the Geneva Book Exhibition: everything leads us to believe that Jacques Neirynck, ex-professor in EPFL (Swiss Federal technology University), has quietly cooked up a best seller again (*The Vassula Enigma,* by Jacques Neirynck). The subject is absolutely astounding and utmost popular: Vassula, the woman who says she writes under God's dictation, gathers together crowds in the whole world and her books are sold by hundreds of thousands. This fifty-five year-old Greek-Orthodox, born in Egypt and emigrated in Switzerland, gives rise to mistrust from Vatican and the Swiss episcopacy. Not from Jacques Neirynck.

The Interviewer: You already wrote a novel on the Shroud of Turin. Now, you are publishing your dialogue with Vassula, who hears heavenly voices. Do you not fear burning your reputation as a scientist?

Jacques Neirynck: I consider that my scientific reputation is not compromised by this book. I am an expert in electricity, not a doctor in psychology. I am also a believer and, I add, instinctively mistrustful when facing supernatural phenomenon. In fact I am a journalist. I have just tried to do an honest work of journalism.

A journalist who has good reasons to be careful that his interviewer would check the veracity of his statements. By being content to re-

transcribe Vassula's replies to your questions, you display a certain benevolence towards her right away.

It is true, I believe that she is of good faith. I was reluctant, when the publisher proposed my meeting her. Had I found myself in front of a delirious hothead, I would have given up. However, I discovered a very reasonable woman. And I realized that what she was telling me sounded very true. Therefore, I felt I had to do this work.

But how can your scientific curiosity be contented by only reporting her statements?

It is true that the topic is far from being exhausted. If one would want to investigate—and perhaps I will do it—there would be many ways. First of all, the analysis of photographs taken by witnesses, showing white halos around Vassula. Then, a new graphological analysis of her two different handwritings: her natural one, and the one called "hieratic," issued from the dictation. What would also be needed, is a comparative text analysis: if Vassula really writes under dictation, the vocabulary and turn of phrases should not be the same. At first sight, the difference is striking. Vassula speaks in a summary way. However, her "inspired" texts contain magnificent passages.

Reading the book, one thinks immediately of a split personality. Would you think Vassula is schizophrenic?

I am not a specialist, but she looks way too calm to be a schizophrenic. A psychologist told me that such phenomenon occur with autistic children: they are completely walled in, and suddenly they start to speak, sometimes in an unknown language. Or with upmost precision they draw a building they just happened to pass through. Undoubtedly, There is a double state of consciousness in Vassula. But getting rid of the case by decreeing that it is a mental illness, is really depreciating. One could say that Joan of Arc was a schizophrenic, and yet one would not have said anything of her.

You are comparing her to Joan of Arc?

Yes, absolutely. Like her, she is an ordinary woman, who is not part of the church machinery. This fell on her without her asking for it. And it gives rise to the same mistrust from the ecclesiastical hierarchy. Her message is traditional, she extols obedience to the pope, but that's it;

she is a woman, an Orthodox, a foreigner, divorced, then remarried. She gathers crowds and calls Christians to unity. It is disturbing.

Nevertheless, as you say, Vassula's conformism is astounding: she sees Mary with blue eyes, paradise like a cathedral dome, the angels and the purgatory...
It is true, her visions are very traditional. She speaks to ordinary people; this is what the Church is no longer able to do with its cold and boring liturgies.

Do you believe that God is speaking to Vassula?
I believe there exists an invisible world and that, sometimes, people enter in contact with it. The phenomenon is well known in the history of Christianity. It happens that when God reveals Himself, He does it through very modest people, who have nothing to do with the Church organization.

If Vassula's charisma is true, what is her mission?
Our churches are emptying. Vassula, for her part, succeeds in gathering eight hundred people in a suburb hall, just for praying. She does nothing else, but she replies to a fundamental need of the human being; to pray is a physiological necessity, almost like making love! I feel that this woman deserves tolerance from the Church. If the latter closes its doors to her, people risk going to pray elsewhere, in gatherings which would not necessarily be very Catholic.

Vassula's Presentations

1988—Lausanne

1989—**Switzerland:** Saint-Maurice, Geneva, Delemont, Montreux, Friborg, Martigny, Courtetelle, Jura, Lusanne; **France:** Biarritz

1990—**France:** Albi, Marseilles, Mazamet, Auch, Nice; **Switzerland:** Broc (4), Lens, Saint-Maurice, Sion, Martigny, Villars; **Italy:** Milan, Torino

1991—**Switzerland:** Geneva, Villanova, Lens (5), Martigny (5); **Italy:** Pistoia, Milan, Gera Lario; **France:** Toulouse, Boust, Besancom; **Canada:** Montreal, Chateauguay, St. Hyacinthe, St. Georges Est, Quebec; **Ireland:** Athenry, Dublin, Belfast; **U.K.:** Carfin, Auchinleck, Ayrshire, Manchester, York, Beckenham, Balham, London; **United States:** Kansas City area, Pittsburgh; **Belgium:** Brussels

1992—**Switzerland:** Villanova (6), Geneva (3), Glariers, Porrentruy, Lusanne; **Australia:** Camberwell, Adelaide, Melbourne, Doncaster, Saint Albans, Bondi Beach, Sydney, Merrylands, Annandale, Carina, Brisbane; **Philippines:** Manilla; **Japan:** Akita; **France:** Ars, Versailles, Paris, Nice, Haut-Rhine; **Italy:** Rome, Verona, Genoa, Florence, Gera Lario, Milan; **Russia:** Moscow; Portugal: Requiao; **Greece:** Rhodos; **Germany:** Wallenhausen; **Mexico:** Matzalan; **Belgium:** Brussels; **Canada:** Ottawa (4); **United States:** Orchard Lake, Pontiac, Warren, Mt. Clemens, Highland, Livonia, Wyandotte, Hollywood (Fla) (9), New York, Independence

1993—**United States** (2): Notre Dame, Sacramento, Los Angeles, Santa Clare, Omaha; **Switzerland:** Geneva (World Council of Churches), St Gall, Villanova; **Mexico** (3): Guadalajara; **Martinque; Portugal:** Lisbon, Evora; **France:** Paris, Lorient, Gex, Arles; **U.K.:** Glasgow, New Castle, Manchester, Staplehurst; **Israel:** Jerusalem, Bethelem, Tel Aviv; **Canada:** Chicoutimi, Quebec, Edmonton, Winnipeg; **Philippines:** Cebu; **Greece:** Rhodos, Athens; **Denmark:** Copenhagen; **Sweden:** Stockholm; Norway; **The Netherlands:** Heiloo; **Zimbabwe:** Harara; **Malawi:** Blantyre, Lilongwe; **Zambia:** Lusaka; **Italy:** Rome, Florence, Milan; **Russia:** Moscow (7); **South Africa:** Pretoria, Johannesburg, Durban; **Haiti:** Porto Prince

1994—**Canada** (8): Ottawa, Toronto; **United States** (8): San Francisco, Stockton, South Carolina, Notre Dame, Greensville, Gaithersburg, South Hadley, Waterbury, New York, Manhasset; **Italy:** Milan; **Greece:** Athens; **Romania:** Iasi; **Switzerland:** Villanova, Geneva; **France** (10): Laval, Dijon, Caen,

Rennes, Bordeaux, Pau, Thierenbach, Sauvian, Marseilles, Gex, Toulouse; **Puerto Rico:** Santa Montana, Manati; **Haiti; Mexico; Columbia:** Nabia; **Ecuador:** Quito; **Brazil:** Joinville, Sao Paulo, Recife; **Portugal:** Requiao; **Argentina:** Buenos Aires; **Chile:** Santiago; **Peru:** Lima; **U.K.:** London, Sussex, Birmingham; **Poland:** Poznam, Chorzow, Varsovie; **Germany:** Essen

1995—**Israel** (8): Jerusalem, Bethlehem, Jifna, Ramallah, Iblin, Melia, Nazareth, Haifa, Beir Zeit; **U.K.:** London; **Switzerland:** Lusanne (4), Geneva; **Spain** (6): Santa Cruz, Bilbao, Sevilla, Madrid, Barcelona, Palma de Mallorca; **Netherlands TV; Uruguay:** Montevideo; **Argentina:** Buenos Aires, Mar de Plata, Saint Michael of Tucuman; **Italy:** Ragusa, Gera Lario, Napoli, Rome; **Canada:** Peterboro; **Denmark:** Copenhagen; **Sweden:** Stockholm, Goteborg; **Netherlands:** Hilversum; **Norway:** Oslo; **Brazil** (8): San Carlos, Joinville, Curitiba, Brazilia, Maceio, Rio de Janerio; **Panama; United States:** Puerto Rico, Los Angeles; **Japan:** Osaka, Beppu; **France:** Paris; **Austria:** Linz; **Indonesia** (2): Djarkarta; **Bangladesh:** Dhaka; **Belgium:** Beauraing; **Bosnia-Hercegovina:** Croatia, Split, Zagreb, Otok, Djakovo; **Hungary:** Budapest

1996—**Switzerland:** Geneva, Lusanne (5); **Canada:** Montreal, Vancouver; **United States** (19): New York, Lakeland, Goose Creek, Rockville, Washington, D.C., Atlanta, Indianapolis, Minneapolis, St. Louis, Phoenix, Las Vegas, Wauwatosa, Los Angeles, Denver, Boerne, San Antonio, Milwaukee, Seattle, San Francisco; **Sweden:** Stockholm, Goteborg, Malmo; **Ireland:** Dublin, Limerick; **Poland:** Tychy, Olsztyn, Varsovie; **Germany; Egypt** (8): Cairo, Alexandria, Maadi, El Zeitoun; **Belgium:** Kortrjik; **Spain** (7): Barcelona, Las Palmas, Murcia, Madrid, Seville, Bilbao

1997—**Switzerland:** Lusanne (6), Bale, Geneva; **Spain:** Madrid; **Germany** (11): Barlo, Numbrecht, Munchen, Fulda, Berlin, Stolberg, Cloppenburg, Norderstedt, Konigstein, Augsburg; **Austria:** Bregenz, Wien, Salzburg; **Belgium:** Brussels; **France:** Laval, Toulouse, Nice, Paris; **Brazil:** Joinville, Puerto Alegre, Curitiba, Fortaleza, Vicosa, Brazilia, Campinas; **U.K.:** Belfast, Cardiff, Abington; **United States:** Ashton, Elmhurst, Allston, Greenville; **Japan** (13): Shibuya, Yokohama, Tokyo, Kobe, Sapporo, Osaka, Salesians; **Israel:** Jerusalem, Nazareth, Haifa, Tantour; **Italy:** Milano; **Netherlands:** Hetogenbosch; **Philippines:** Manila, Cebu; **Indonesia:** Jakarta; **Canada:** Prince George (2); Vancouver

1998—**Venezuela:** Caracas; **United States:** San Francisco, Denver, Houston, St. Louis, Pittsburg, Lakeland, Minneapolis, Chicago, New York; **Canada:** Ottawa, Shawinigan, London; **France:** Lyon, Gex; **U.N.; Italy:** Rimini; **Argentina:** Buenos Aires, Salta; **Uruguay:** Montevideo; **Germany:** Freiburg, Saarbrucken, Langerwehe; **Slovania:** Ljubjana; **Switzerland:** Lusanne; **Greece:**

Athens; **Israel:** Jerusalem; **Australia:** Hobart, Melbourne, Sydney (4); Papua **New Guinea:** Port Moresby, Boroko; **Thailand:** Bangkok; **Peru:** Lima; **India** (16): Bombay, Cochin, Alleppy, Mangalapuzha, Manickpur, Chicalim, Vasco da Gama, Margao, Panaji, Muringoor, Kottayan, Palai; **Philippines:** Quezon City, Mandaluyong, Kamunig, Manila; **Bangladesh:** Dhaka

   1999—**Venezuela:** Caracas, Coro; **Columbia:** Duitama; **India** (13): Mumbay, Alleppey, Bharananganam, Athirampuzha, Manarcaud, Kollam, Muringoor, Edappally, Margao, Panjim, Calcutta, New Dehli; **United States:** Pittsburgh, Brooklyn; **Sweden:** Gallivare, Stockholm; **France:** Le Mans; **Greece:** Rhodos, Syros Island; **Bangladesh:** Dhaka; **Japan:** Toyko, Fukuoka, Heroshima, Kobe; **Russia:** Moskva; **Lebanon:** Hamra, Beyrouth; **Switzerland:** Lusanne; **Brazil:** Puerto Alegre, Florianopolis, Lauro de Freitas, Sao Jose dos Campos, Belo Horizonte, Vitoria, Rio de Janerio; **New Zealand:** Aukland, Hamilton, Hastings; **Thailand:** Bangkok, Ampher, Si Swasda; **Lesotho:** Maseru; **Zambia:** Lusaka, Kabwe; **Kenya:** Nairobi

   2000—**Romania:** Bucharest, Oradea; **Puerto Rico:** Cayey; **Italy:** Rome, Benevento; **Jordan:** Amman; **Lebanon:** Bsalim; **U.K.:** New Castle, Edinburg; **Greece:** Athens; **Lesotho:** Roma Valley, Maseru; **South Africa:** Johannesburg; **Benin:** Cotonou; **Kenya:** Nairobi; **Israel:** Bethelem

   2001—**Mexico:** Mexico City; **Puerto Rico:** Caguas; **India:** New Dehli; **Bangladesh:** Dhaka; **Sri Lanka:** Colombo; **Czech Republic:** Prague; **Greece:** Chania, Heraklion, Sounion, Athens; **United States:** Brooklyn; **U.N.; Italy:** Camponogara (Venice); **Israel:** Jerusalem, Nazareth; **Singapore:** Singapore; **Australia** (7): Perth, Alice Springs, Adelaide, Melbourne, Camberra, Gold Coast, Sydney; **Papua; New Guinea:** Port Moresby, Buka, Mt. Hagen; **South Africa:** Johannesburg, Soweto; **Swaziland:** Matsapha, Manzini; **Malawi:** Lilongwe, Blantyre (5)

   2002—**Cambodia:** Phnon Penh; **China:** Hong Kong; **Taiwan:** Taipeh; **Philippines:** Manila, Cebu; **Egypt:** Cairo; **Mexico:** Guadalajara, Merida; **India** (12): Bangalore, Kalyan, Mumbai, Muringoor, Chalakudi, Mundoor; **Sri Lanka:** Colombo, Kandy; **Germany; Switzerland:** Lusanne; **Chili:** Santiago; **Venezuela:** Caracas; **Canada:** Lethbridge; **Netherlands:** Amsterdam; **South Africa:** Soweto, Houghton, Johannesburg, Pretoria (radio); **Italy:** Spinea, Feletto Umberto